NEVER *feel* UNLOVED *again*

NEVER
feel
UNLOVED
again

*Symptoms and Strategies
to Cure Low Self-Esteem*

COACH RATNER

Copyright Notice

© 2024 Coach Ratner. All rights reserved.

No part of this book may be reproduced, distributed,
or transmitted in any form or by any means,
including photocopying, recording,
or other electronic or mechanical methods, without
the prior written permission of the publisher, except
in the case of brief quotations embodied in critical
reviews and certain other noncommercial
uses permitted by copyright law.

Book cover & interior design by:
Joanna & Grzegorz Japoł - LUNA Design Studio

Table of Contents

Start Here	7
The Symptoms of Low Self-Esteem	**13**
1. Imposter Syndrome	14
2. Avoiding Social Interaction	19
3. Poor Relationships	22
4. Self-Destructive Behaviors	26
5. Hypersensitivity	29
6. Comparing Yourself to Others	31
7. People Pleasing	38
8. Perfectionism Leading to Procrastination	40
9. The Emotional Can Turn Physical	43
10. Fishing for Compliments	46
11. Fake Confidence	49
12. Criticizes Others	53
13. Likes to Gossip	56
14. Tattoos, Bull Nose Rings, and Plastic Surgery	58
The 4 Ways You May Contribute to Low Self-Esteem in Others	**65**
1. Name Dropping	67
2. The Humble Brag	70
3. Pressuring Others	72

4. Posting on Social Media	75
The 12 Strategies to Cure Low Self-Esteem	**79**
1. Forgive The Source	80
2. Be Happy With Internal Satisfaction	88
3. Controlling Your Exposure, Emotional Vampires and Critical Thinking	93
4. Discovering and Living With Your Core Values	102
5. List of Attributes	108
6. Rejection Therapy	111
7. Familiar and Comfortable Are Not The Same	115
8. Set a New Goal For Yourself	126
9. Make Life Fun	131
10. Synchronize With Others	136
11. Exercise	138
12. Meditation and Prayer	142
Author's Notes	176
About The Author	179
Preview of Sunscreen Love	**182**

Start Here

**"The greatest prison we can put ourselves in
is worrying about what other people think of us."**

In 2021, the Centers for Disease, Control & Prevention, also known as the CDC, released a staggering report that one out of every three teenage girls had seriously contemplated committing suicide. This is based on interviews from 17,000 teenagers. The rate for boys is half of that, which is interesting in the way that they published the report. You could understand this report to mean that the rate for boys contemplating suicide implies acceptability, or downplays its significance.

Imagine teaching a classroom of 30 teenage boys and finding out that five of them are thinking about suicide. You would think there is something in the water or air that is poisoning them. This still represents an alarmingly high number that warrants attention.

For high schoolers that have actually attempted suicide and not just thought about it, the numbers are astounding.

Ten-percent of youth in grades 9-12 reported that they had made at least one suicide attempt in the past 12 months.[1] I don't know about you, but these numbers are even hard to grasp.

The prevalence of this issue has reached epidemic proportions. While it's crucial to recognize that not all instances of suicide attempts or contemplation stem solely from low self-esteem, addressing the root of the problem is imperative. Encouraging individuals to cultivate self-love could significantly alter the landscape. The alarming surge in the usage of antidepressants serves as a stark reminder of the severity of this crisis.

I don't know anyone that has not gone through periods of life where they have had low self-esteem, but not to the extent we are seeing today.

When does the issue with low self-esteem start? Usually it occurs during and after puberty and can persist until our twenties and beyond. For many, it's when their mother asked them to put on a wool winter hat before going outside on a frigid winter morning. Most of us have no problem doing it in 3rd or 4th grade. However, a shift occurs as self-consciousness settles in. Wearing a wool winter hat to the bus stop suddenly feels awkward, and creates a fear of appearing socially undesirable in the eyes of your peers. Looking like what we think is a geek in front of students of the opposite gender is then outweighed by the discomfort of freezing our ears off.

The greatest prison we can put ourselves in is worrying about what other people think of us. This can be one of the most limiting and suffocating experiences in life. When we become preoccupied with seeking external

---

[1] According to the American Foundation for Suicide Prevention, based on the most recent Youth Risk Behaviors Survey from 2021

validation and approval, we allow the opinions of others to define our self-worth and happiness. If we don't get those opinions that give us that validation, then this can lead to a cycle of anxiety, unhappiness, and of course, low self-esteem. Freeing ourselves from this mental prison involves a journey of self-discovery and acceptance.

Our hope is that we will outgrow the feeling of low self-esteem and we will eventually be happy with ourselves, paving the way for self-love. Regrettably, this hope does not materialize for many. Because of that, the struggle with low self-esteem continues into our adult life. No one wants to have the feeling of being unloved, by others or by yourself. If you don't love yourself, it will be a difficult task to love others.

I have navigated through phases of low self-esteem in various stages of my life. Unfortunately, for a long time, I did not have the clarity to seek help or educate myself about it to overcome these struggles. Now that I do have clarity, I want to turn my mess into my message.

> *"I want to turn my mess into my message"*

For those grappling with low self-esteem, my aim is that by the time you reach the end of this book, you'll find yourself on the path towards building positive self-esteem. If you're fortunate enough not to battle with low self-esteem, I hope the insights within this book become a valuable resource in assisting those around you who may be struggling. Additionally, if you're dealing with clinical depression, consider using this book as a supplement to therapy and medication, working together towards a journey of happiness and joy.

Low self-esteem is not something that the Social Security Administration considers a disability. It does not fit into their criteria for financial assistance like they do with other disabilities. However, the long-term problem with low self-esteem is that it has the potential to manifest itself as a physical ailment. The correlation between emotional well-being and physical health is reflected in that the happiest people tend to live the longest lives. Our emotional and physical states are intricately connected and can have a profound impact on our overall health.

Low self-esteem is somewhat similar to darkness. Darkness does not exist. It is just an absence of light.

What is the speed of light? About 186,000 miles per second. What about the speed of darkness? It doesn't have one—because darkness isn't something that moves; it's just what's left when the light disappears.

Even the early narrative of the Bible starts with "darkness upon the surface of the deep" right before the famous words, "…and let there be light." It is obvious that darkness was there before creation and the Bible even tells us that. How could anything have existed before creation? It didn't, because it does not exist.

Black is not a color. Which means, any low self-esteem that someone has, in theory, does not exist. It is just an absence of light that has permeated the life of someone with low self-esteem. However, try telling that to someone with low-self-esteem and they will probably throw a soda can at your head.

If low self-esteem does not exist, you may need to change the vision of how you see yourself. By altering your mindset, you have the power to transform your entire life. Your city of happiness only resides in one place; your state of mind. If you can change your mindset, you can change your life.

*"Your city of happiness
only resides in one place;
your state of mind"*

The ultimate goal of this book is to bring light back into your life. Much like a small candle can light up an entire dark room, I hope that this book will serve as the spark that brightens up your soul, guiding you out of the dark place that you may find yourself in. Ultimately, I will unveil my 12 strategies that will infuse light back into your life. If you are not happier after reading this book than when you started, then I have failed, and I have no intention of failing. Your well-being is the driving force behind every word. I am not writing this book for anything or anyone else, but to help you.

You may look at yourself just like a raw diamond: rough around the edges, maybe a bit oddly shaped, full of irregularities and imperfections. A raw diamond that is transformed through precise cutting, with the correct angles, shape and size, is one of the most beautiful objects in the world. Its beauty is based on its ability to allow light to permeate it and reflect its brilliance back out.

You are just like a diamond in the rough brimming with untapped potential. All that is required is careful reshaping of your mindset to allow the light to permeate your soul. What is exciting is that you may be the most beautiful diamond in the world, but your low self-esteem is hiding your inner brilliance. When you finally overcome your low self-esteem, you will recognize the dazzling person that you are. You will then spread that brilliance back out to the world and discover that there are *many* people who love you. You will then *Never Feel Unloved Again.*

The Symptoms of Low Self-Esteem

This chapter aims to highlight symptoms that may be indicative of having low self-esteem. It does not mean that experiencing any of these symptoms conclusively indicates a struggle with low self-esteem. Just like having a cough and sore throat doesn't necessarily mean you have COVID-19—it could be a common cold, strep throat, or another ailment. These clues are just indicators that you may be dealing with the potential of having it.

If you find yourself resonating with several of these traits, there's no cause for panic. Many individuals encounter these challenges at different points in their lives. Understanding these symptoms is crucial for your emotional well-being. Awareness will help you navigate these feelings, cultivating a greater understanding of what you need to do to maintain happiness in your life.

1.
Imposter Syndrome

This is when you doubt your skills, talents, and accomplishments and you have a fear of being exposed as a fraud. It affects individuals across various stages of their careers and expertise levels. The term "syndrome" can sometimes imply a more severe or clinical condition, but imposter syndrome is not a mental disorder; rather, it is a psychological pattern of self-doubt and fear of being exposed as a fraud, despite evidence of competence.

This syndrome is not relevant for someone who is just in the beginning of a new path in life, because you may really be a bit of an imposter. The syndrome of being an imposter is relevant for someone who is just average in their skill level, or someone who is at the top of their game, what you would call an expert in their field.

Comedians often grapple with the challenge of taking the stage, wondering if the audience will think their material is funny. It's only once they hear genuine laughter from the audience that their self-assurance begins to resurface.

Courtroom attorneys may have doubt in presenting arguments before a judge. Their confidence may waver initially, but as they present their case, their self-assurance tends to strengthen.

It also may be the rookie quarterback who was a star in college and now struggles in the professional league. They may be an excellent quarterback, but the intensely higher speed of the professional game versus college is too much for them. The combination of imposter syndrome and the quickness of the game lends to the fact that few rookies are able to reach their potential. It is also one of the reasons that so few rookie quarterbacks can start in the National Football League, or why evaluators of talent have such a difficult time drafting successful quarterbacks.

It may be a female model who feels like she is ugly and does not like herself. If you think back to your high school days, you might recall a girl that was considered beautiful, yet never acknowledged your existence or of anyone else in your social circle. Although she was always called "stuck-up", she might have been exceptionally shy or struggled with low self-esteem. Your perception of her beauty likely shaped assumptions about her confidence, whereas if she were merely average-looking, you might not have labeled her as stuck-up and probably would never have given her a moment of your thoughts.

It may be you, who's an expert in something, but you may even struggle to gain confidence because you think you may be a fake. It is only when you have done something over and over for many years, when you feel confident that you are not a phony. It is when you have positive self-esteem that you clearly recognize that you know what you are doing, without feeling that you are an imposter.

Occasionally, experiencing a touch of imposter syndrome can be a catalyst for achieving skills beyond comprehension even if they are considered at the pinnacle of one's field. There's a compelling argument that suggests this is essential for those regarded as the greatest of all time.

Despite Tom Brady getting his fifth Super Bowl victory, which sealed his legacy as the GOAT, the **G**reatest **O**f **A**ll **T**ime, he may have grappled with imposter syndrome. This sense of self-doubt could have propelled him to elevate his game to unprecedented levels, defying age norms and securing a remarkable 6th and 7th Super Bowl ring, a feat once deemed unattainable.

Michael Jordan consistently faced challenges throughout his career, starting from the disappointment of being cut from the varsity high school basketball team to being labeled a below-average defender after his rookie year in the NBA.

Whether you label it a "chip on the shoulder" or a touch of "imposter syndrome," that motivating factor propelled Michael Jordan to relentlessly practice, ultimately leading him to become not only the greatest basketball player in history, but the best defender the game has ever seen. Which may irk some people because without the defender status, he would still be considered the GOAT.

Imposter syndrome tends to be the most damaging when you find yourself in the middle of the talent spectrum. It's often when you're merely average in a particular area that imposter syndrome can negatively impact your self-esteem.

Here are five tools to get over imposter syndrome:

1. Set realistic goals because you don't have to accomplish everything all at once. The race to the finish line isn't won by the first person out of the gate. It is slow, steady, consistent work that will improve

your talents and skills. If you're a rookie in anything, you'll have to slowly get over imposter syndrome. If you are average as far as talent, set realistic goals and you won't have to deal with imposter syndrome. If you are a superstar already, use the imposter syndrome you feel to get even better and to surpass what may be already recognized as great. You are already an outlier, so don't let it bother you too much.

2. Define what success means to you, because if you don't, someone else will do it for you. Then you may have been successful in life and completely missed it. This will help you avoid imposter syndrome.

3. Stay away from toxic competitions where winning is so important. Michael Jordan only won 6 championships out of 15 seasons. Were those other 9 seasons a failure? Of course not! You will *not* win most of the time, so don't feel like an imposter if you don't win or are not #1 in your field.

4. Don't rely exclusively on external validation for your self-esteem. Have confidence that you are an expert in what you are doing, even if no one else recognizes it.

5. Don't let your job define who you are as a person, unless your job is so meaningful beyond the financial reward that you want it to define you. Set limits and boundaries to avoid overworking. Maybe you feel like you are not qualified for your job and feel that you are an imposter. Understand that this is just how you make a living, not the person you are to your friends, family, and loved ones. Your job should define what you do for a living, not who you are.

One should refrain from boasting about personal achievements and attribute success to others whenever feasible. This concept reflects the virtue of humility. Practicing humility serves as a powerful antidote to imposter syndrome, fostering an awareness that one's skills and talents are bestowed gifts that one utilizes to the best of their ability.

Picture a scenario where a member of an elementary school PTA single-handedly puts together a highly successful fundraiser. Instead of taking all the credit, she praises the other board members, despite them doing very little. This act of humility involves reducing the focus on herself and acknowledging the efforts of others. Someone with the highest levels of self-esteem does not worry about receiving accolades, rather, their humility signifies a mindset that allows one to share credit without seeking recognition. Being humble is not thinking less of yourself, but thinking less *about* yourself.

> *"Being humble is not thinking less of yourself, but thinking less about yourself"*

When one has strong self-esteem, the need to claim the credit diminishes, and a willingness to share the honor will increase. Even when everyone knows that the project succeeded because of one person, individuals with strong self-esteem opt to distribute credit, potentially inspiring others to take on more responsibilities in the future. With this in mind, recognizing imposter syndrome as a symptom of low self-esteem, one can learn to deflect praise and realize that any feeling of being a "fake" is not justified.

2.
Avoiding Social Interaction

Can you recall a student in college who always stayed in their dorm, even on weekends, while you were out going to bars and parties? You might have perceived them to be boring. However, one factor to consider is that they may be an introvert, finding joy in solitary activities like reading or studying. Their definition of fun simply differed from your definition of fun. This does not necessarily indicate low self-esteem; rather, it reflects on their preference in how they derive satisfaction; reading a book in their dorm room on a weekend is fun for them, even though it may not be fun for you.

There is a fine line between someone who avoids social situations because they are an introvert, versus someone who doesn't like being in social situations, because *they are scared out of their minds!* The latter may have anxiety and have a constant fear of being judged. These individuals may think they are ugly or unworthy of conversation; plagued by fears that deter them from going into any social interaction.

Sometimes, individuals might label themselves as introverts when, in fact, their avoidance of social situations stems from low self-esteem. This may manifest itself in a reluctance to engage with others, driven by their belief that they are not capable to be loved, or able to be loved by someone else. In this scenario, making excuses to avoid social interactions becomes a way of sidestepping their deeper issue and their self-imposed introvert label is being used as a protection from facing their reality.

This is similar to some individuals who may claim they don't want to get married, not because they have no interest in marriage, but because they recognize they might not be capable of being in a loving relationship. This declaration of not wanting to be married becomes a convenient excuse to avoid confronting their emotional flaws. The prospect of putting themselves in a position to love someone else may uncover their emotional deficiencies, which they want to avoid. Acknowledging these issues requires vulnerability, something they find challenging so they make an excuse to evade the truth altogether. Then they live their entire life with this internal contradiction.

On the other hand, attempting to engage in a romance while carrying low self-esteem might lead to disastrous outcomes or, at best, a somewhat dysfunctional relationship. The choice between confronting personal challenges or avoiding them altogether shapes their relationship choices.

It's more constructive to acknowledge your faults and address them directly. Granted, this process involves vulnerability which many find uncomfortable. This discomfort is why some individuals choose to avoid social interactions altogether. The fear of putting oneself "out there" for everyone to see, becomes a powerful deterrent, leading them to steer clear of socializing entirely.

3.
Poor Relationships

Imagine if I told you that I have someone that would be a great match for you, but then told you that they struggle with low self-esteem. Chances are, you would pass on going on a date with them. No one likes to be with someone that is not happy or does not love themselves. Unfortunately, many people are not aware that this is an issue when they marry. This is a major reason why there are so many poor relationships. One should be careful when dating someone with what appears to be confidence, but is masking low self-esteem.

In advising single men struggling with dating, I often emphasize the importance of confidence, a trait highly sought after by women. Striking the right balance is crucial – not overly confident, as it may come across as arrogance, but rather exuding a strong, quiet confidence. Just to clarify, I am a man, or what currently classifies as a man, and it is possible that I am incorrect about women desiring confidence, but so far, no one has questioned me about it.

When you have strong self-esteem, it shows in how you interact with other people, and usually someone who has strong self-esteem will be more successful in their job or business. This confidence also translates into effective parenting because they will minimize the impact of emotions and anger on their parenting approach. If you have children and have yelled at them, you probably realize that unleashing frustration on them yields no positive outcomes and can even make the situation worse.

Navigating a relationship where one partner possesses strong self-esteem while the other grapples with low self-worth can be challenging. The individual with low self-esteem may harbor the belief that their partner could never truly love them, leading them to sabotage the relationship. This struggle is a personal journey I experienced during my own dating experience.

I was dating what I thought was a smart, beautiful, confident woman. While my observations about her were somewhat accurate, it turned out that she was masking low self-esteem. This became apparent as our relationship deepened and she struggled to accept love. She started making self-defeating comments like "you can't love me" and "why are you with me." This was a new and challenging experience for me, by a long shot.

If I had been more mature and wise at the time, I might have recognized that these behaviors stemmed from deep-seated issues of low self-esteem. Unfortunately, lacking that insight, I responded in a way that's probably very common for most men — I broke up with her. The dilemma was that she did not want to allow the breakup, yet she couldn't prevent herself from undermining it. The situation escalated to the point of stalking and threats of suicide.

Thankfully, she eventually sought therapy, which proved to be successful. Over the years, she learned to love herself and eventually found a lasting relationship, leading to marriage. This experience underscored the importance of recognizing and addressing underlying issues of low self-esteem in relationships.

A considerable number of individuals might refrain from investing the effort needed to improve their self-esteem, potentially leading them to remain single, or in poor relationships, for their entire lives. The fundamental premise is that loving yourself is a prerequisite for being capable of loving someone else. Later in this book, you'll find 12 strategies aimed at addressing and overcoming low self-esteem, providing an excellent starting point for loving oneself.

When individuals who are dating seek a potential partner, they may unknowingly gravitate towards someone who shares similar flaws. This stems from the comfort of recognizing aspects of themselves in another person. While these characteristics might not be consciously sought, encountering someone with the same flaws creates a sense of comfort and connection.

I've observed couples where both struggle with low self-esteem, and while it's not the ideal scenario, it can work with counseling and therapy. The journey to a successful marriage for such couples often involves a significant investment in personal growth.

My wife and I once knew a couple who appeared to have an ideal marriage, and their separation left both of us in shock. While both of them were exceptional individuals, it became clear that they might not have been ideally matched. The wife revealed that she had bypassed relationships with seemingly perfect guys because they lacked a flaw that she identified in herself. It was only after marrying her husband, and raising a family together, that she recognized that she picked her husband because they had shared the same flaw. She then reflected on why she had passed up on such exceptional men before she chose her husband. She realized that her own low self-esteem caused her to feel she did not deserve such an outstanding guy. Because she thought of herself as a flawed individual, she felt she only deserved a flawed individual.

As the demands of real life set in, the nuances of everyone's imperfections become more apparent. When individuals claim that their dating or married partner is perfect, it often raises a red flag that they are overlooking the inevitable flaws. There is no one who is perfect, but there is someone who is perfect for you.

If you have low self-esteem, it does not preclude the possibility of having a fantastic marriage. You just need to enter into a marriage having clarity with all your issues. Be aware that you may choose someone because they have the same flaws, and that should be a warning sign that you should proceed with caution.

4.
Self-Destructive Behaviors

Has there ever been a time in your life when you thought you were invincible? For many people, it was probably during their teenage years and into their mid-twenties. People are always looking for stimulating, hair-raising adventures. That's why extreme sports and roller coasters are so popular. Obviously these are thrilling, but the deeper reason why people do them is that it makes them feel alive! The true appreciation of being alive is when you go through something where the slightest mishap would kill you.

We willingly invest in experiences that carry an element of danger—be it skydiving, hang-gliding, or surfing giant waves. Much like the delicate balance between having low self-esteem and being an introvert when steering clear of social interactions, a similar nuance emerges in thrill-seeking activities. It becomes crucial to discern whether the pursuit of thrills is driven by a desire to feel alive, or not caring if you die.

Navigating this demands true introspection, prompting individuals to question their motives for taking risks. Achieving clarity with this issue may be tough since individuals may hesitate to confront uncomfortable truths about themselves. One's ego may not let them admit that they don't care about dying, unless they are in a very dark place.

When you don't love yourself, you are more willing to take risks. People with strong self-esteem can also die from dangerous behavior, but the difference is that they *don't want* to die. They are just doing it for the adventure that makes them feel alive.

When you have strong self-esteem, one tends to avoid perilous situations, especially when others depend on them. Raising children serves as a powerful antidote to low self-esteem. Their presence shifts the focus from one's own needs and feelings to caring for the well-being of others, reinforcing a sense of responsibility.

You may recall someone from high school or college who never missed a chance to be at a party—a student perpetually getting drunk, chugging beer bongs, liquor shots, illegal substances or anything dangerous that was offered to him. This individual might have frequently blacked out, gotten into fights, or damaged property. This behavior as the party guy often serves as a signal compensating for low self-esteem.

How often have we come across stories of young men driving recklessly at high speeds during the late hours, tragically dying after crashing into a tree? Some of these individuals might have grappled with low self-esteem, allowing them to take unnecessary risks because they feel a lack of self-love. Other perilous behaviors include illegal drug use, playing with dangerous weapons, or indulging in unprotected physical relations with multiple partners.

Self-destructive behaviors are obviously a sign of potentially worse issues than just low self-esteem. Knowing how to identify the differences between someone not caring if they die, versus someone *wanting to die,* can ultimately save someone's life by getting them the proper intervention. This is why recognizing and helping someone with low self-esteem in its early stages can guide them toward a healthier path, potentially averting more severe consequences.

5.
Hypersensitivity

Have you ever woken up in the morning and you found yourself staring at a pimple right in the middle of your nose? Your immediate reaction might be to decide not to leave the house, fearing embarrassment if someone were to see it. This feeling of potential embarrassment is just that, it's our feeling and not rooted in reality. Someone with strong self-esteem would realize that most people don't pay much attention to your pimples. Your best friend may playfully tease you for a brief moment, but it's likely they won't even notice it after a few seconds. In general, a pimple is generally not as significant to others as it may feel to you.

Do you find yourself spending extensive time ironing your clothes, styling your hair, or constantly worrying about your appearance in different outfits? This level of preoccupation with our appearance would diminish if we had stronger self-esteem.

During my travels, I used to pack several nice dress shirts and would spend about 30 minutes ironing them upon reaching my hotel. Then, one day, I witnessed my best friend ironing his shirts, and it only took him a mere 15 seconds for each! His approach involved a single pass on each sleeve and each side of the shirt's front. Intrigued, I asked, "That's all you iron?" His response was an eye-opener: "95% of the wrinkles are out, and the rest won't be noticeable anyway." I then realized that my extensive ironing was rooted in my hypersensitivity to how I perceived others saw me.

It's important to clarify that one should not abandon efforts to look polished and put together. Taking pride in our appearance is a positive practice. However, for some individuals, a preoccupation with looking flawless can become paralyzing. This sensitivity can be indicative of low self-esteem. Striking a balance between presenting oneself well and not being overly fixated on any imperfections is crucial for a healthier self-image. If you happen to have teenage girls, you know exactly what I am talking about

6.
Comparing Yourself to Others

Do you find yourself constantly watching your competitors? Is your attention fixated on them instead of concentrating on your own achievements? We can go through life enjoying contentment from our own successes or perpetually watch others and constantly compare. This is particularly evident on social media, where some influencers will proudly brag that they have reached a million views on TikTok or Instagram. Boasting about your number of views on social media is like bragging about how much money you have in Monopoly; it holds no real world significance unless you can turn Park Place and Boardwalk into actual real estate. How you value yourself should not be based on an algorithm that randomly replays your videos to a million people.

True value in social media lies in meaningful engagement: likes, shares, subscriptions, and the impact your content has on its viewers.

Individuals with robust self-esteem don't feel the need to resort to comparisons. They recognize the positivity in their message and its potential to contribute to the world. Their contentment stems from this alone. While getting to this level of self-esteem may seem a bit far-fetched, the goal of this book isn't for readers to live with average self-esteem, but to raise your self-esteem higher than you can dream! This means having a mindset where the only one you are comparing yourself to, is you.

> *"...the goal of this book isn't for readers to live with average self-esteem, but to raise your self-esteem higher than you can dream"*

Drawing comparisons with others has the potential to lead you to abandon your goals. Looking back, there are some invaluable lessons I learned from instances where I gave up on a dream. If I had access to a book like this over 40 years ago, it might have prevented me from quitting on myself. While we are certainly not seeking out challenges, their impact on shaping us into better individuals becomes evident only in hindsight.

During my high school years, I was exceptionally good at playing the piano. I thought that I was so good that I contemplated pursuing a career in the music industry with a dream of playing on Broadway. I decided to apply to the top two music schools in the country: the Oberlin Conservatory of Music in Ohio and The Juilliard School in

New York. The TV show "Fame" was very popular during that period, which was based on the struggles of students at Juilliard. It was my favorite show, and the prospect of attending Juilliard would have been a dream come true.

During my junior year of high school, I received an invitation to perform at a County Music Festival in Virginia. When I arrived at the school for the first time, I headed straight to the room filled with pianos where all the accompanists would practice. What I witnessed was amazing and depressing at the same time. The room was brimming with high school kids playing piano at a level that I had never seen before. They played classics by Chopin, Gershwin, and Rachmaninoff, as well as contemporary pieces by Billy Joel and Elton John. While I could also play the same music, their skill level was beyond anything I had seen before. They could play by ear, which is playing any song on demand without any music, and also change the key at will. I was good, but not *this* good. This left me a bit bummed out about my prospects as a professional pianist. Imposter syndrome reared its ugly head because at this point I *was* an imposter in my own eyes.

At this time in my life, I was secluded between my high school, family, friends, and my synagogue. This constituted my social circle and, at the time, my entire world—and it was great! I received praise for my piano playing anywhere I played, which led me to believe I was among the best piano players in the world. This warped perception of how good I was arose because I had very little exposure to anything outside my world. So in my eyes, I was the best. That was until I got out of my world.

Eventually, when I came across all these exceptionally talented pianists, my dreams of pursuing a professional career in piano not only went out the proverbial window, I also decided to not apply to Oberlin and Juilliard. It was a devastating blow, one that, in retrospect, should never have occurred. Why did I not believe in myself and still apply to those schools? Because I compared myself to others and it caused me to not believe in myself. Not only will comparing yourself to others cause you to have low self-esteem, it may cause you to abandon your dreams.

This experience has imparted a couple of crucial lessons. Firstly, success in life doesn't demand being the best at something. It just requires being good enough. One should know that no matter how good they are at something, someone will end up surpassing you. The pursuit of success should be based on continual improvement rather than fixating on being the best.

There are many ways that a talented musician can make a living. I just compared myself to students who were likely prodigies, headed for careers playing classical music for major symphonies. While I may never possess their talent, I had other talents that may have led to my success. I could have written popular music, played in a band, or even entertained guests on cruise ships or restaurants.

When someone gives up without even trying, it robs them of the opportunity to discover and pursue alternative paths. I never gave myself that chance.

Another crucial lesson learned from this experience is one should silence negative thoughts, especially from themselves. Oftentimes, we emerge as our harshest critics and our own worst enemies. This self-sabotage can become a barrier to personal growth and can prevent healthy self-esteem. This can lead to regret and can damage your self-worth.

There are 2 kinds of regret in the world. One is where you attempted something and failed. The other is the regret of never trying it at all. This latter regret has been with me for me the rest of my life—never knowing what I could have composed, produced, or what joy I might have brought to the world. This regret has stemmed from comparing myself to all the other pianists in that room. I came to the realization that stopping the habit of comparing oneself to others leads to a more fulfilling life. It tears away self-doubt and frees one from feeling inadequate.

One should recognize the difference between comparing yourself to someone more accomplished than you versus striving to achieve their same level of success. Comparisons can be valuable only when used as a source of inspiration. However, understanding that mirroring someone else's path to success doesn't necessarily mean you will have the same journey. Everyone's journey and approach to their level of success is completely different.

Challenges arise when the pursuit of someone else's personal goals transforms your feelings into inadequacy and low self-esteem. To avoid falling into this trap, one should just use others' accomplishments as inspiration, not actual goals. A strategy to prevent low self-esteem is to acknowledge that you are observing these achievements as goals for personal growth. Insert a crucial "but" to yourself, emphasizing that you won't let it lower your self-esteem if you haven't attained the same milestones.

I should have come to the realization that I may never have the same technical skills of the other pianists. However, I should have continued to work on my craft and enjoyed the ride to whatever success I achieved. Instead, I just took all of the piano playing out of my future. It did not have to be an "all or nothing" endeavor, but that is exactly what I did; I turned my potential success into nothing.

Low self-esteem can be pronounced in communities where the emphasis on personal growth is lacking. If this is an issue where you live, your bar for success may initially yield a false sense of accomplishment. This is because you are basing your success on those around you. When people have strong self-esteem, they do not look at the successes of others. They are continually improving themselves, unswayed by benchmarks of those around them.

Consider the scenario of checking out your neighbor's lawn. You may find it comforting thinking to yourself, "At least my grass isn't four feet high; it's only one foot high." Okay, so you haven't mowed your grass in two weeks whereas your neighbor has not mowed it all summer. In reality, both of you have failed to be responsible. However, this kind of comparison becomes problematic when extended to other aspects of life, such as personal conduct. If you're evaluating your actions against someone who constantly cheats on their spouse with the maid and nanny, and you're excusing your behavior by saying, "I only cheated once with my secretary," you have set a low bar for yourself.

We may also do this when we go to a restaurant and someone else at the table orders dessert, while we decide that we are already full and don't really want anything else to eat. Since they order it, you feel the urge to go along with them and order one for yourself. This is obviously a simplistic example, but a good analogy to think about in more important aspects of life.

Comparing individuals who engage in questionable or unethical behavior can lead to a distorted view of oneself. True personal growth involves setting standards that are not only higher than the immediate surroundings, but also aligned with your core values and principles. If you have to compare yourself, it's essential to choose comparisons that contribute positively to one's character.

The concept of "Keeping Up With the Joneses" involves maintaining a similar standard of living as those within your social circle, including neighbors, friends, and families associated with your children's school. This practice can be positive when the Joneses engage in activities like charity work or helping those in need. That kind of pressure is good for all of us. However, if the Joneses' lifestyle involves private jets, 2nd homes, and secret lovers, attempting to keep up with them may lead to feelings of low self-esteem.

A more constructive approach is to completely eliminate low self-esteem from your life by eliminating any comparisons to others. Instead, focus on your core values. The true measure of success lies in aligning your goals with your values, rather than attempting to match someone else's success. Otherwise, you might be frolicking on your lawn with your nanny through four feet of grass while eating a chocolate dessert that you don't really want.

7.
People Pleasing

Why can people pleasing be a symptom of low self-esteem? Occasionally, the desire to want to help people may not be totally altruistic, but from a diminished sense of self-worth. You may feel the need to help people to gain approval and validation.

I often encounter the question: "Isn't it good that I want to help people?" Absolutely, yes! However, one must discern the motivation behind helping others. There exists a fine line between offering assistance out of genuine kindness, or doing so to seek positive reinforcement to raise one's self-esteem. If one were to select a symptom of low self-esteem, this is for sure the one to have to manage.

I once knew a woman in college who displayed immense kindness to everyone around her. She was constantly organizing birthday parties and buying gifts for people she barely knew. Reflecting on it 40 years later, it became apparent that her kindness and thoughtfulness stemmed from deep-seated low self-esteem. Despite being an incredible person, she remains unmarried, possibly still dealing with negative thoughts about herself. It's hard to love someone else when you don't love yourself, even though she *is* loved by many. It is a great quality to want to help other people, but one should determine the source of your kindness. If not, you may make poor decisions, especially when you are in the early stages of a romantic relationship.

When there is physical intimacy very early in a relationship, it's conceivable that one partner is grappling with low self-esteem and that fulfilling the other person's desires will make them feel accepted. Unfortunately, this is quite common and it is wise to be aware of it if you are dating. That way you won't confuse love with infatuation and then find yourself in a toxic relationship later on.

I know people who would *not* take a relationship seriously if the other party wanted to have physical relations with them after one or two dates. People pleasing is a good trait to have when it comes from your good nature, *not* when you are looking to get approval from someone else. Your personal desire to date them to mate them may turn into a situation where you date them and then hate them. You just have to ask yourself which side of that fine line you are on when people pleasing, *especially* when it comes to dating.

> *"Your personal desire*
> *to date them to mate them*
> *may turn into a situation*
> *where you date them*
> *then hate them."*

8.
Perfectionism Leading to Procrastination

You may say to yourself that whatever you want to do will never be perfect, so why should you start? This is what someone with low self-esteem is thinking in their minds, either consciously, or subconsciously. This reluctance to even start something may stem from past experiences of criticism, which can significantly diminish one's self-esteem. This serves as a valuable lesson for anyone involved in any relationship — excessive criticism can discourage people to take any risks or start anything altogether.

Procrastination can keep you from embarking on starting a business, beginning an exercise program, pursuing a degree, or maybe even getting married. Did you ever tell your mother, "why should I bother making my bed, it's going to get messed up again anyway?" This attitude will doom you to never going anywhere in life. I really want to write that it will doom you to failure, but how you can fail at something if you never try it. Failure means you, *at a minimum,* attempted something. It is those who don't fail because they never took any risk that may be worse off in life. They may look at themselves as a failure, but really what they are is a procrastinator.

Getting back to the grass analogy, there is a famous saying, *the grass is always greener on the other side.* This proverb means that the neighbors' grass is greener and if I had what they had, I would be much happier. In reality, what it really means is that when you look straight down at *your* grass, what do you see? You see dirt. From your perspective, your life (and yard) is full of dirt because you can see *through* the grass. When you look at your neighbors' grass, what are you really looking at? You are looking at the *lush side* of their grass. From your angle, you can't possibly see any dirt from afar like you do looking down at your own grass. Your perspective is completely different from theirs. When they are looking at your grass, they don't see any of your dirt either. They are thinking the same thing as you! If I only had *their grass,* I would be so much happier. It means you think your situation is poor, dire, impossible to deal with and you think your neighbor's grass is perfect. In reality, your struggles may or may not be more difficult than your neighbors', but it is *your* struggle. If it is given to you, it is because you can handle it.

This is a common faulty view in marriages that are going through some turbulence. Some spouses would prefer someone that did not have a particular challenge that they have to deal with. In this situation, what they may not realize is that if they think that switching to a new spouse will make them happy, then all they are doing is switching one challenge for a different challenge. They may view a new spouse as having greener grass, when in reality, it's just a different problem that they may have a harder time coping with.

This illusion of seeing your neighbors' perfect grass can put a stranglehold on your life and keep you from starting anything. You don't want to become an expert in procrastination. Your struggles are given to you because you have the strength to overcome them.

In numerous instances, we may not be fully aware of other people's struggles. Take, for instance, those neighbors whose marriage appears perfectly happy. It can be disconcerting when your own marriage doesn't seem as content. What often goes unnoticed is the possibility that there are hidden troubles and the looming possibility of divorce that we don't even realize.

Many of us are familiar with that guy from high school who sold his tech company for tens of millions of dollars. It's natural to feel a twinge of jealousy, especially if you considered yourself smarter back in school. What may not be apparent is that he may be grappling with substantial debt or, worse, struggling to navigate newfound wealth, potentially leading to a downward spiral involving drugs and gambling. The key lesson here is not to let the perceived success of others deter you from pursuing your own endeavors. Understand that your attempts may not always work out the way you want, but don't allow that thought process to hinder you from starting something meaningful.

Put an end to procrastination, and you'll find that low self-esteem will dissipate from your life. It's crucial to understand that no matter whose grass you observe, if seen from their perspective, there's always dirt. No one's grass is flawless, and yours won't be either. Enjoy your grass and realize that no matter how many times your grass is cut, it always comes back stronger, and you will too.

9.
The Emotional Can Turn Physical

When exploring the lives of individuals who have lived to a very old age, a recurring theme is often their contentment and happiness, not their wealth. This holds true even for those who have endured significant adversities such as poverty or war. While not always explicitly acknowledged by many doctors, there exists a correlation between emotional stress and the manifestation of diseases.

"Stress doesn't only make us feel awful emotionally," says Jay Winner, MD, author of "Take the Stress Out of Your Life" and director of the Stress Management Program for Sansum Clinic in Santa Barbara, Calif. "It can also exacerbate just about any health condition you can think of."

According to WebMD, studies have found many health problems related to stress. Stress seems to worsen or increase the risk of conditions like obesity, heart disease,

Alzheimer's disease, diabetes, depression, gastrointestinal problems, and asthma.

During a recent business trip, I had the opportunity to talk with two individuals whose stories highlighted the paradox of wealth and stress. One encounter was with an old client who confided in me about the strain caused by customers failing to pay their invoices. Despite managing an impressive $300 million in annual sales, he found himself always having to handle the burden of collecting debt. He boasted about his ten-percent profit margin, while at the same time complaining about unpaid invoices and his poor health. In case math is not your strong suit, that ten-percent margin means he makes $30 million a year.

I also crossed paths with a major donor to a non-profit organization during the same trip. This individual, who owned many hotels in New York City, seemed stressed by the pressures of his business. Despite his abundant wealth, the anxiety from managing his empire made what should be a happy old man into a cranky old man. When a health challenge eventually makes its way to him, he will have a hard time recovering from it due to his anxiety over his business.

These encounters served as reminders of the intricate relationship between wealth and well-being. While financial success can open doors to comfort and luxury, it also has the potential to cause anxiety and turmoil if not managed wisely. It's a realization that even among the most affluent, stress can persist, serving as caution for us all to focus on inner peace above material accumulation.

When you have money, you may spend more of your time acquiring possessions and taking vacations. The more money one has, the more you have to manage it.

The more possession you have, the more you have to manage them also.

This is why if you are one of those people who are careful about taking care of their physical body, you should also take care of your mental health. When your mental health falters, or when you think you really can't control your negative feelings, that can manifest itself into the deterioration of the physical body. They go hand in hand. This is why when you see people who are very overweight, there is usually an emotional reason why they are overeating, and it's not because they are more hungry than you. Overeating serves as a coping mechanism for underlying unhappiness. A more beneficial alternative, as explored later in the chapter on exercise, is redirecting emotional struggles towards activities like running.

I believe that many doctors will refrain from telling their patients a timeline of how long they have to live when diagnosed with a deadly disease. It is their understanding that conveying such prognoses can impact the emotional well-being of individuals, which then shapes their reality. Our thoughts can create reality and if you feel unloved or have low self-esteem, that emotional feeling can turn into a physical malady.

10.
Fishing for Compliments

I am blessed to be able to speak for various organizations around the world. Before I used to be aware of my self-esteem, I would ask for feedback from the person who invited me. It finally dawned on me that I was just essentially fishing for compliments. Like most people, I enjoy receiving compliments. The realization that this behavior stemmed from my own low self-esteem prompted me to make a change. I became more conscious of the significance of cultivating positive self-esteem, without the need for external validation. I now prefer them to arise naturally, without me having to ask someone else.

One challenge I grapple with is that no matter how proficient you are in whatever you do, not everyone will resonate with your message. Looking back on my speeches in Maryland many years ago, I estimated that I talked to around 300 different individuals over the years. Whether in small classroom settings or larger events like the Jewish High Holidays, this spanned across numerous years. From my perspective, approximately 10 individuals stood out as genuine fans of mine. These were people who actively sought out my talks, purchased my books, and passionately recommended me to their friends. While 10 may seem like a small number, the realization struck me when I considered extrapolating that percentage across millions of people.

This epiphany motivated me to continue with writing and speaking, even though I felt I was not garnering a large enough audience.

Here are some unmistakable signs that someone is seeking compliments:

1. Openly boasts about their accomplishments or wealth
2. Pretends to show ignorance about their positive qualities, hoping that someone will remind him
3. Says negative things about themselves to bait you into saying something positive about them

Regardless of how well you performed your job, unless it was outright dreadful, fishing for compliments often results in receiving a positive response. People will hesitate to tell you directly that you stunk. Instead of fishing for compliments, consider that if you did a remarkable job, feedback will likely come from the sponsoring organization or other indicators. Perhaps there's a noticeable uptick in book sales or a surge in new subscribers to your website or podcast. These outcomes serve as more reliable indicators of your success without the need to solicit feedback from others. You may even get asked to come to perform again.

We engage in this behavior of fishing for compliments frequently, especially through social media. Consider the impact on your self-esteem when you post something and receive zero likes or comments. You probably don't feel great about yourself when this happens.

There is also an idea about being self-deprecating. This is when one is excessively modest or even disparages themselves. They may be doing this to invoke reactions that lead to a compliment, which is just another way of fishing for compliments.

Aspiring to have strong self-esteem requires refraining from fishing for compliments in situations where judgment is possible. Instead, carry yourself with confidence and pride, recognizing that you've given your best effort, regardless of others' opinions. In any pursuit, no matter how well you perform, there will always be individuals who may not appreciate your efforts. It's essential to acknowledge that it's impossible to please everyone. So leave the fishing to the fisherman.

11.
Fake Confidence

Have you ever encountered someone who initially struck you as incredibly confident, only to discover upon getting to know them better that it was merely a facade?

My initial encounter with such a person took place during the early stages of my career in the rare coin business. At the time, I was around 17 years old and grappling with imposter syndrome, possessing enough knowledge to engage in the trade, yet lacking the confidence to fully embrace that I knew what I was doing. At a convention in Maryland, I crossed paths with a young man around my age who exuded an air of self-assurance. He bragged to me about his past trading successes, emphasizing that he exclusively dealt in the finest coins. In other words, he was cocky. His demeanor aimed to make me feel small, which I did.

A decade later, when our paths crossed again, I discovered that he had long departed from the coin business, and much of his once-prominent bravado had dissipated. It became evident that what had initially seemed like genuine confidence was, in fact, a facade. This individual had been harboring what I now refer to as "fake confidence."

I've come to realize that those who boast the most often tend to harbor the least confidence. True confidence doesn't necessitate constant self-promotion; when you're genuinely secure in your abilities, there's no need for excessive bragging.

In nearly everyone's life, there's often that one individual who consistently takes center stage. Most likely it is someone you knew back in high school or college. This person has a knack for entering a party with a raucous remark that grabs everyone's attention. When someone is planning a social gathering, he's the first name that comes to mind because he's universally acknowledged as the one person you need to have a successful party. In reality, it is just covering up for his lack of positive self-esteem. This is his way of feeling accepted and gaining attention for himself.

This behavior is often observed when you come across a group of teenagers strolling down the street. Occasionally, there's a young individual who makes a deliberate effort to be loud—whether through expletives, loud sounds, breaking beer bottles, or even knocking over objects like a trashcan. In these instances, it becomes apparent that they are seeking attention.

I dated a woman many years ago that displayed the perfect example of the phenomenon of having "fake confidence." I met her at a singles mixer when I was in my early 30s. She was cute and full of life! She was extremely confident in herself, not in an arrogant way. She was the exclusive agent for the rights to a famous folk hero. It was an unusual profession for a young woman and I found it to be very intriguing. She probably found my job fascinating since I was a coin dealer; something that very few people understand, or have heard of. That fun and exciting relationship lasted about 1 month until the demons started rearing their ugly head. What was originally confidence, turned into a horrendous display of complete distrust, low self-esteem, and irrationality.

Her troubled past remained concealed initially. It just took time for the confidence to fall away and reveal the true essence within her. It reminds me of the TV show Survivor as an example of how hard it is to hide your emotional problems for too long. At the end of every episode, someone gets voted off the island and the game is over for them. At the show's outset, contestants are interviewed and express their intentions to become better versions of themselves, or hide certain aspects, such as severe insecurities, or wealth, which will usually cause you to get voted off. This facade usually crumbles pretty quickly. Living in close quarters for an extended period of time makes it difficult to maintain a false identity.

It seems that it is hard to hide your truest self when you are living amongst other people. This is why there are many divorces where one spouse says that they were completely surprised by the negative emotional state or dysfunction of the person they married. This is usually very soon after the wedding; even just a few days!

Wealthy contestants can successfully keep this hidden aspect of themselves under wraps for a significant portion of the show. Conversely, those characterized by deceit, sneakiness, or emotional instability are typically revealed very quickly, within the first few days, or even hours of the competition.

The woman I was dating was able to attract me because I was not able to see through the veneer of her fake confidence. It was only when *she* could not keep it hidden any longer that I became aware of the dysfunction. It was a good lesson for me to always be aware of when the air of confidence is masking a troubled past.

Exercise caution when encountering individuals whom you perceive as overly confident; their outward appearance may merely mask underlying feelings of low self-esteem. Additionally, ask yourself whether your own confidence truly reflects your authentic self or serves as a cover for hidden insecurities.

12.
Criticizes Others

What if I told you that there is a new yoga instructor at your gym who is highly critical? Would you want to meet them? Chances are you would say no. After all, nobody enjoys being around individuals who constantly criticize others. Where does the need to constantly criticize come from? It is possible that the origin of it is linked to low self-esteem. When you criticize someone else, it could be a reflection of your own dissatisfaction. It is an attempt to elevate yourself by bringing others down. This is not the route you want to take in life if you want to feel good about yourself.

Looking back on what made me a mess, I finally came to acknowledge that I used to be very critical of many people in my life. It's possible to go through life without recognizing this trait within oneself, as it can become ingrained in one's personality without realizing it is an issue. It may take someone you trust to bring it to your attention. I am blessed to have a practical and sensible wife who gently pointed it out to me. Once I became aware of my critical nature, I made a deliberate effort to refrain from it. So much so, I composed a little song that I sang throughout the day called "complement, don't criticize." This has been a game changer in our marriage because I am now constantly aware of it.

My father used to criticize my brother all the time when we were little. My brother, not being the most graceful person in the world, occasionally spilled his drink at the dinner table. My father did not take into consideration that he was clumsy and it was part of his nature. The constant yelling and criticism likely took a toll on my brother's emotional well-being over the years. Now that I have children, some more coordinated than others, I refrain from yelling when one of my children inevitably spills their drink. I just tell them to go get a towel and clean it up. I make no reaction of any kind, especially disappointment. I want my children to take responsibility for their actions, even their mishaps. My aim as a father is to nurture positive self-esteem in my children, fostering confidence as they go out into the world.

I have noticed that children who have had a positive emotional connection with their parents tend to navigate the loss of a parent more effectively. In contrast, I've witnessed the challenges faced by children who lost a parent with whom they had a strained relationship—they often grapple with the aftermath for an extended period and have a tremendously tough time getting over it. This sometimes stems from parents who were overly critical. On the other hand, children with emotionally healthy connections to their parents, while still experiencing sorrow at the loss, demonstrate a quicker resilience and ability to bounce back.

In a marriage where one spouse constantly criticizes the other, it often signals underlying issues of low self-esteem, which could lead to potential trouble. If you find yourself in a dating situation where your partner frequently criticizes you, it's a red flag that should not be ignored. In such cases, it might be wise to consider permanently stepping away from the relationship to preserve your emotional health.

One of the fundamental principles for successful relationships is offering compliments instead of criticism. Every time you criticize someone, you are tearing them down emotionally. Every time you compliment someone, you are making them feel good about themselves and also fostering positive feelings towards you. Realizing that constant criticism is a potential sign of low self-esteem will hopefully be a catalyst to help you to become a person that everyone wants to associate with. Just ask yourself if you want to be around someone who radiates happiness and compliments instead of criticizes. Chances are you will say yes, unless you are an emotional mess.

13.
Likes to Gossip

Why is gossip a symptom of having low self-esteem? Someone who is not happy with their life will get pleasure gossiping about someone else. They may be also compensating for their unhappiness by talking about the problems of other people to avoid their own problems, or it makes their problems not seem as bad. That is why when someone gossips, they may say 'what's the lowdown' or 'what's the dirt' on someone else. It is because you are dragging someone else through the mud because it makes you feel like you are clean.

For example, if you like to talk about who is getting divorced in your neighborhood, you probably don't have a strong marriage yourself. When you have strong self-esteem, you do not need to bring anyone else down or talk about their problems to make yourself happier.

Gossip involves 3 people: the speaker of the gossip, the listener, and the one who is being spoken about. Gossip includes saying anything about someone else that is true, untrue, or even if you use negative body language or facial expressions when someone speaks. The most common one is the eye roll. Even if you say that you would tell whatever it is you are saying to someone's face, it is still considered gossip. Even if you say I am not sure this is gossip; it's most likely gossip.

Gossip can be harmful because we always don't know the reason for someone else's issues. Gossip can also just be speculation, which can eventually harm someone. There are entire books on gossip, but the purpose here is not to discuss all the ways gossip is harmful. It is just for someone to realize it may be a symptom of low self-esteem.

It is similar to a satellite that is in orbit looping around the earth. Gossip is a bit similar. We may say something that can travel around our social circle and eventually harm someones relationship or reputation. **S**peaking **A**bout **T**he **L**ives **O**f **O**ther **P**eople is an acronym for SATLOOP. Just like a satellite loops around the earth for many years, but it will eventually burn up or crash into earth. Your gossip will do the exact same thing.

When you gossip about someone else, it can spread like wildfire and eventually damage someone's reputation. When you live with internal happiness, you have no need to speak about the lives of other people.

14.
Tattoos, Bull Nose Rings, and Plastic Surgery

In this chapter, I'll be addressing a topic that may stir controversy, particularly among those who have made certain choices concerning their bodies. I am writing this knowing full well that I will have to defend myself and may cause some people to feel insulted. My goal is not to be liked, but to provide insights to help you reach your potential in life! If that takes me telling the truth and possibly cause feelings to be hurt, I will suffer the consequences.

You can always tell when a young person is going through emotional turmoil. It can manifest in the way they dress that may seem uncivil to many adults. They may have many earrings in body parts that are not their ears, vibrant neon hair colors, and various body modifications, such as tattoos. While I respect the diversity of these choices, it may be that it is all based on an inner struggle from having low self-esteem. This is not a judgment on their choices, but the emotional reasons that have caused them to make those choices. This is just a generalization and not every person with tattoos has low self-esteem.

Tattoos have become a common form of artistic expression, but the skin plays a role in protecting the body and it is also our largest organ. I am not sure that you would ever consider putting a tattoo on your 2nd largest organ, the liver, even if it was possible to see it. Tattoos can have side effects, such as inflammation of the skin, several forms of hepatitis, and can negatively affect your immune system over time.

A tattoo stands in stark contrast to the sudden urge to purchase the latest sparkly pink sundress because Taylor Swift wore it at her recent concert. Unlike clothing that can be given away or sold at a clothing reseller, a tattoo becomes an enduring part of your identity. It is not so easy to get rid of. Body art can cause regret, emphasizing the need for strong consideration before committing to something so permanent.

When one does not love themselves, they want to do what they can to start to feel better as fast as possible. You feel bad about yourself, so you end up at the tattoo parlor. In these instances, tattoos emerge as a cheap and quick means of affecting a physical change in one's life. This is a case where the body art compensates for not taking mind-altering drugs and you end up completely covered in tattoos. However, if you want to feel really expressive about your low self-esteem, you take mind-altering drugs *and* get a body full of tattoos.

If you don't love yourself, you may not care if you damage yourself. If you do love yourself, would you even consider damaging your largest organ? Some people are going to respond that tattoos are not that damaging. Maybe they are only slightly damaging, but the issue extends beyond surface-level concerns.

Research indicates that getting a tattoo can be indicative of self-destructive tendencies. This correlation prompted a search into the psychological aspects of getting something that is so permanent.

Henry J. Carson, a clinical pathologist and medical examiner from Linn County, Iowa, undertook a comprehensive study that involved examining cases from his county and neighboring ones.[2] Only adults 18 years and older were included in the survey. Tattoos are typically noted on a coroner's report so Carson compared the data of deceased persons between tattooed and non-tattooed.

Out of a total of 438 deaths, 300 had no tattoos, while 138 people had tattoos. The median age of death for those without tattoos was 53 years, and those with tattoos, 39 years. What should be noted from the survey was that since no one under eighteen years old was included, the median age for tattooed deaths is probably skewed higher than what it truly is since young people are more likely to have tattoos.

The association of being tattooed and relatively early death by any manner was striking. However, the presence of a tattoo doesn't serve as a predictor of early death, but rather may represent an epiphenomenon, a secondary symptom occurring simultaneously with a disease or condition, but not directly related to it.

The association between having tattoos and risk-taking behavior has long been observed clinically, especially with people who obtain tattoos at younger ages. There is evidence that persons with tattoos are significantly more

---

[2] A 15 year study from 1997-2012

likely to use illicit drugs, drink excess alcohol, and are more likely to die from these causes.

What this report is speculating is that if you get a tattoo, you are probably not thinking of the possible consequences of your actions in all aspects of life. Someone who has strong positive self-esteem probably isn't sketching permanent ink into their skin, therefore, tatting yourself might be a symptom of having low self-esteem. This is just a theory and more data would need to be examined if the data from Linn County reflects the country as a whole. But there is a new trend now that is fortunately not as permanent as tattoos, but may be a larger symptom of having low-self-esteem.

Bull Nose rings in the septum have always been used on cows to help them wean themselves from their mothers. It has now become a fashion statement to look like a cow. The only reason I can come up with why young men and women want to look like a cow is that they have no idea they look like a cow. If they knew that cows have earrings placed in the septum of their nose to help stop them from breastfeeding, then wearing a nose ring may be more than a fashion statement. The link between the cow's nose ring and the potential self-esteem implications remains speculative, especially since many individuals might be unaware of this association.

Generally, young adults who are always following the latest fads are looking to be accepted by their peers. This is probably an issue with almost every teenager in the world, but it can be a real problem when it is associated with a number of other symptoms of low self-esteem.

I once read an online article from an American magazine about how models in some European countries pose with hairy armpits. What was striking were the comments about how most women thought it was gross. I thought to myself that if any popular celebrities were posting pictures of themselves with hairy armpits, then it would suddenly become en vogue. Imagine Taylor Swift raising her arms at MetLife Stadium with hairy armpits. I don't think it's a far fetch that almost every teenage girl would quit shaving their underarms. Fads help us feel like we are being accepted by our peers, where in reality, we are just not thinking for ourselves.

The most dangerous and permanent predictor of having low self-esteem is cosmetic surgery, sometimes known as aesthetic or plastic surgery.

Does the decision to undergo breast augmentation surgery, or any elective cosmetic surgery equate to having a symptom of low self-esteem? Delicately put, yes. Obviously if you are having cosmetic surgery to replace a body part that was lost or damaged due to cancer or any other cause, then it is not elective surgery.

Now that I am close to 60 years old, I do scrutinize myself in the mirror and think that if I just tighten the skin on my neck a tiny bit, I would look 20 years younger. Then I think about all those men in their 70s & 80s who look funny because of the disparity between the smooth skin on their faces and their arthritic appearance. It becomes evident that the attempt to erase wrinkles can sometimes create an unintended contradiction with the natural aging process; tight skin and creaky bones that just don't quite harmonize. Or to say it another way, they look weird.

Years ago, I was in Palm Beach, Florida, jogging along a path that ran along the scenic intracoastal waterway. In the distance, I noticed a woman approaching. Judging from the silhouette of her body, I assumed she was a young woman in her twenties. However, as she got closer, I was shocked to realize that she was well into her 70s.

The sight was so jarring that my mind struggled to reconcile the discrepancy between her age and the perkiness of certain body parts; it just did not look right.

Isn't it possible to age naturally and be happy with the way we look? In a world influenced by media-driven beauty ideals, the pressure to conform to unrealistic standards has led many to consider cosmetic surgery. The impact of marketing has probably caused some people to go under the knife fueled by a desire to emulate the ageless Tom Cruise or Cher. It's noteworthy that Cruise, in his 60s, continues to maintain a remarkably unchanged appearance since his role in "Risky Business" over four decades ago, setting unrealistic standards for aging gracefully.

Sharyn Osborne, wife of Black Sabbath vocalist Ozzy Osborne, and a judge on America's Got Talent, openly acknowledges undergoing a series of cosmetic procedures. Her reported enhancements include facelifts, Botox injections, dermal fillers, lifts for both her legs and arms, a tummy tuck post-gastric-band surgery, breast implants, and a neck lift.

The television personality mused in her 2013 autobiography: "Every time you go under the knife for vanity, you are slicing off yet more of your self-worth." Still, in 2021, she had more surgery on her face, something she now sees as "the worst thing that I ever did." She said she had the procedures because of vanity and ego. "Oh, you look great for your age, but I know what I really look like. When I look in the mirror, I see the real me."

Regardless of the number of tattoos, bull nose rings, or breast enhancements that someone has that resemble a topographical map of Mount Everest, everyone has moments of feeling like a mess. Let's delve into some approaches to genuinely boost self-esteem, or else you'll spend a lot of plastic just to end up looking like plastic.

The 4 Ways You May Contribute to Low Self-Esteem in Others

While individuals are ultimately responsible for their own self-esteem, we have tremendous potential to affect how other people feel about themselves. However, the most important reason for understanding this concept is to create awareness for ourselves. Understanding how we affect someone else's self-esteem will help us have a better understanding of what affects our own self-esteem.

You have probably encountered someone who left you feeling uplifted and great after your interaction with them. What made that experience so gratifying? In this chapter, we will explore how our actions and words can significantly influence the self-esteem of others. While individuals with strong self-esteem may not be affected by our words or actions, unfortunately, this is not the case for many people.

The way we present our face has an affect on people we interact with. How often do you see your own face? As a man, you might catch glimpses of it around 3 or 4 times a day, while for a woman, it's probably more frequent. However, the people you interact with daily—your friends, co-workers, and family—see your face constantly. Therefore, how you present yourself can significantly impact those around you.

A smile is a powerful tool; it can uplift others and create a positive atmosphere. When you choose to smile, you often trigger a chain reaction, making others smile in return. Smiles are contagious, and by sharing a cheerful expression, you spread joy to those you encounter.

In contrast, wearing a pouty or negative expression may have the opposite effect, affecting the mood of those around you. Being mindful of how you present yourself can enhance your relationships and create a more pleasant social environment.

This is a journey of self-improvement is one that we can all embark on. Writing this chapter helps me gain clarity on what I need to do, or not do, to be happy. It's a reminder of the kind of person I want to be - someone who spreads positivity and uplifts others.

Just as I wrote books about marriage to cultivate an awesome relationship, this journey towards self-improvement is a way to nurture and enhance my own well-being. By focusing on how we interact with others, we contribute to creating a more positive and compassionate world, one smile, and one kind word at a time.

1.
Name Dropping

How do you feel when someone engages in name-dropping around you? Name-dropping involves mentioning someone's name that you know, even if the connection is more tenuous than you let on, all in an attempt to boost your social standing in the eyes of others. It provides a momentary sense of importance, but it's not a sustainable way to build genuine self-esteem. This tactic may be a quick fix to elevate how you feel about yourself, but it's fleeting because it lacks authenticity. The reason it fades so rapidly is that the association with the mentioned person is often superficial. Since the connection is not deeply rooted, your internal compass recognizes the insincerity, leading to a potential erosion of your self-esteem, leaving you feeling worse off in the long run.

If you genuinely have a close relationship with someone of importance and find yourself wanting to mention their name, it's advisable to be cautious unless it is for a specific purpose. Using someone else's name solely to elevate your social status in the eyes of others may leave you feeling as if you're exploiting that connection. Unless there's a legitimate reason to bring up their name in a certain context, refraining from name-dropping prevents the impression that you're leveraging relationships for personal gain. It's similar to the experience of someone using certain drugs—there's a fleeting sense of euphoria, but once the effect wears off, there's that lingering hangover that feels miserable.

There is another similar concept to name dropping that is a particular pet peeve of mine. It is what I call the "You don't know so and so? Everybody knows so-and-so!" phenomenon. This occurs when someone mentions a person they know, assuming that you should also know them. This individual could be a local celebrity, a social media personality, or even a Rabbi. The issue here is the expectation that you should know them, leading to a sense of inadequacy if you don't. What they may overlook is that your social circle may be entirely different from theirs. Personally, I've always recognized the negative impact of such assumptions and have refrained from making that comment. Unfortunately, there are certain people who lack the wherewithal to understand they are dropping the "you don't know so and so?"

This phenomenon of making assumptions of who you know seems to be challenging with individuals that exhibit traits similar to Asperger's syndrome. This may be someone who is *slightly* on the spectrum without being formally diagnosed. While they may not meet the official criteria for Asperger's, their social behavior can still be awkward. They do not have the awareness to know that not everyone knows everyone that they know.

For some, recognizing subtle social cues comes naturally, while for others, it may require more effort and practice. Recognizing that individuals may vary in their social awareness can lead to more compassion and a better understanding of each other. When you are aware of the social awkwardness of others, you will less likely let others affect your self-esteem, even though they have absolutely no idea they are doing it to you.

2.
The Humble Brag

Robert Glazer, CEO of Acceleration Partners and the Friday Forward, says the humble brag is when someone makes a seemingly modest, self-critical, or casual statement that is meant to draw attention to one's impressive quality or achievement. The humble brags often seem innocuous enough in the moment, but they can become insincere when you hear them repeatedly from the same person. You start to wonder whether or not they have low self-esteem. The real problem is when they may cause you to have low self-esteem.

Some examples are:

"I missed my flight and had an 8-hour wait at the airport. Fortunately I am a Platinum frequent flyer which allows me to use the airline's private club with access to a hot shower, a place to rest and a great dinner."

"Despite not sleeping all night out and not taking a shower, I noticed guys still hitting on me at the bar."

"During my travels I accidentally spilled wine on my suit. Thankfully, there was an Armani store nearby and they kindly replaced my suit."

Here is the thing about the humble brag: while it's often done in an attempt to sound less boastful, research has shown that it is more oft put than if someone just plain bragged about themselves. It is because it seems insincere. As it turns out, humility and self-promotion don't mix well. We are better off separating the two in our communications, especially on social media. If you want to highlight your accomplishments or abilities, just be upfront about it. Weaving the bragging in between moments of humility doesn't fool anyone—if anything, it makes the humility ring false, rather than making the bragging sound softer.

While everyone needs to promote themselves from time to time, our accomplishments are typically more impressive when we allow them to speak for themselves. Someone who is secure and has strong self-esteem does not need to do the humble brag. They can certainly keep the humble brag out of their conversations to help prevent others from developing low self-esteem.

3.
Pressuring Others

Have you ever found yourself pressuring others to accompany you to events or parties they didn't want to go to? It's essential to recognize that such behavior might be a reflection of our own lack of self-esteem, while at the same time potentially impacting someone else negatively. Understanding why we fear going someplace by ourselves can lead to a deeper understanding of our own happiness. (Although this is not the case when taking personal safety into consideration, such as woman traveling alone at night.)

Perhaps it stems from a fear of being judged negatively. By cultivating a strong sense of self-esteem and finding joy in being by yourself, we can break free from the need for constant companionship. This is also a major requirement to having a highly successful marriage. Loving yourself is a prerequisite to wedded bliss.

When faced with the prospect of attending any event, such as a movie or party, I used to rely on finding someone to go with me. However, as I entered my twenties,

I began to feel comfortable with the idea of going to such gatherings alone. This comfort with doing activities by myself probably stemmed from the many times I used to eat alone while traveling. I understand that not everyone can easily feel comfortable with this approach, as it requires a strong sense of self-esteem to willingly place oneself in situations that many people may be insecure with.

The discomfort of being alone may stem from the perception that having someone else with you somehow validates your presence or makes you feel more socially accepted. This feeling is not uncommon, and it may be associated with concerns about being perceived as a "loser" or somehow inadequate when you are doing activities alone. However, it's essential to recognize that these thoughts are often irrational and not based on reality, but your own personal prison.

Overcoming these feelings of discomfort when alone involves addressing them with a rational mindset. Here are 2 helpful ideas to help you feel comfortable being alone while doing activities:

- **Challenge Negative Thoughts:** Rather than assuming that being alone makes you a "loser," challenge these negative thoughts with positive affirmations. Remind yourself that being independent and enjoying your own company is a sign of confidence and strength, not a sign of weakness. Recognize your worth and value as an individual, irrespective of your social circumstances.

- **Start Small:** If the idea of going to a large party or event alone feels overwhelming, start with smaller gatherings or events and gradually work your way up. This incremental approach can make the process more manageable.

By understanding the roots of your discomfort and taking proactive steps to address them, you can gradually feel more at ease attending events or doing activities alone. Embracing independence and building self-esteem will contribute to a more fulfilling and secure life overall. Then you won't have to pressure others or rely on someone else for your happiness.

If you attend college in an environment where there is a lot of alcohol consumption, you may have noticed that people generally prefer not to drink alone. The perception is that individuals who drink alone may be problem drinkers, as social drinking is often associated while with friends. When someone wishes to drink, but finds no one else in their social group willing to join, they may attempt to persuade others to join them so they don't feel like a deadbeat. In contrast, someone who has already acknowledged their alcoholism tendencies won't face this pressure. They are comfortable with their reality and may not hesitate to drink alone. It's usually those who haven't accepted that there may be potential issues with alcohol that will encourage others to drink with them.

It's essential to understand that pressuring others to join you can potentially cause them to develop low self-esteem. Also realize that projecting our own fears onto someone else highlights how bad our own self-esteem is. Instead, let's respect other people and the choices they make. By doing so, we create a positive environment for everyone involved. You must first figure out why you may not want to go to an event alone. If you realize it is coming from your own lack of self-esteem, you may want to do something to improve it. This may inspire you to try to do something on your own for the first time. This boost of confidence will start on your journey to a greater awareness and improved self-esteem.

4.
Posting on Social Media

It's essential to be aware of how we share aspects of our lives, especially joyous events. You should consider what you want close friends and family to see versus your social media friends. Striking a balance between the two is important to avoid causing low self-esteem in others. While sharing your vacation experiences with your family is natural, it's crucial to be considerate when posting about extravagant activities or expensive vacations on social media with people that barely know you. Being sensitive to people's feelings and self-esteem is a prerequisite for really living with high self-esteem for yourself. Acknowledging that your vacation on a safari is not affordable for most of your social media followers is one way to be thoughtful about how you post. You may say that I am being too sensitive about other people's feelings, and you are right! This book is a guide to help you love yourself and live a happy life, so being sympathetic with other people's feelings is a great start to help yourself.

Recently when discussing this idea with a class of mostly college students, I was bombarded with comments about why should they worry about what other people feel? If someone feels bad about being on social media, then they should get off. Why should I have to worry about what I post?

If you had friends who were not as blessed to have the wealth that you do, would you share pictures of your enormous mansion with them? The same question arises when you know people who have been trying for years to have children with no success. You would probably think twice about how you would share the joyful news that you are about to have another child.

The idea here is to just be aware of other people's feelings, because when you start to have compassion about other people and how you share information, you will be more aware of your own feelings and more likely be a happier person.

I want to be clear that I am not suggesting that you stop posting on social media. What I am suggesting is that one should think about what they post and how it will affect others. Internal satisfaction without the need for external validation is one way to build up your own self-esteem.

When we moved our family to Israel a number of years ago, we started a Ratner Israel chat on WhatsApp. This is where we post pictures of us at the beach or at restaurants with friends. The only people on this chat are our family and very close friends; ones that will not develop low self-esteem if we show our family on a yacht in the Mediterranean Sea, which probably won't happen. Any ill feeling and antagonistic attitudes that we may create will not happen with those closest to us. There is such a thing as causing an evil eye, or jealousy in the world. It is best to not do that by showing off anything that can create it, especially your extravagant vacations, beautiful babies, or brand new Lamborghinis.

A more recent phenomena that has happened because of social media is people posting videos of their gender reveals. It's great that you are having a baby and can't wait for the only real surprise left we have in our life, the gender of our baby. Now it seems that it is proper to announce it to the entire world. Do you have the awareness that there are many people who would do anything to have a baby? Maybe they can't find a spouse to have a baby with, or they have tried for years to have a naturally born baby and have had no success. Your baby is a wonderful blessing and miracle. Certainly share it with your family and close friends, but announcing it to the whole world without the sensitivity that it may cause low-esteem in other people is a lack of awareness.

This is also the same for people who post themselves opening letters from college admission departments. It is great to get accepted to a prestigious school, but this is something that also may cause others to have low self-esteem. Being aware that not everyone can either afford, or has the ability to go to college is one way to be sensitive to other people's feelings, which will help you to be more sensitive and foster positive self-esteem for yourself as a bonus!

The 12 Strategies to Cure Low Self-Esteem

"Be grateful instead of hateful"

A recurring theme to carry forward throughout this chapter is the idea of safeguarding your happiness. Envision creating a protective barrier around it just like a fence in your backyard. Fences serve the purpose of either keeping things in, like young children or dogs, or keeping things out, such as trespassers or wild animals. Just as we deploy safeguards to protect our valuables, money, and loved ones, our happiness deserves a similar level of protection. As you go through life, think about what makes you happy and what causes you to feel bad about yourself. Create your own fence to keep the bad out and keep your happiness in. Put a fence up and protect your most important and valuable asset, your positive self-esteem.

1.
Forgive The Source

Where did your low self-esteem originate from? One likely place might be your parents. How parents act in front of their children has an effect on them for the rest of their lives. Their negative behaviors can have a significant impact on their children's self-esteem. Whereas providing emotional support and encouragement can foster a positive sense of self-worth in children.

A major cause of low self-esteem are people that come from families that deal with dysfunction or have gone through a divorce. There are times that married couples should get divorced, but it does not have to be the high percentage of marriages ending today. I would venture to guess that most parents will say that their children are better off with their parents separated, and they may be right. What you may not hear them say is that their children will develop emotional injuries that may not appear for decades.

Dr. Jane Anderson, a Clinical Professor of Pediatrics at the University of California, San Francisco, states that divorce is detrimental to the emotional well-being of children[3]. Children of divorced parents may experience various challenges. Some of them include:

- Higher risk of emotional distress
- Decreased social and psychological maturation
- Loss in his/her religious faith and practice
- Loss in cognitive and academic stimulation
- Decline in physical health

Other data has shown that children from divorced parents are twice as likely to attempt suicide[4]. They are about 4 times as likely to have trouble fitting in, and I have seen data that shows women who had divorced parents are 60% more likely to divorce themselves and for men the number is 35%.[5]

This is why the biggest decision you will make in your life is who you are going to marry. This is also why I have spent so many years of my life writing and teaching about what it takes to have a passionate marriage. Your poor marriage can have such a detrimental effect on your children if you don't know how to model for them what a healthy relationship looks like.

Children are generally aware that their parents love them, even when they are divorced. It is when the two people

---

[3] Data published in 2014 report from the National Institute of Health

[4] Science Daily

[5] City University of New York

they love the most don't love each other that causes the child to not love themselves. These internal emotional injuries have a tendency to show up later in life, generally *after* they have been married.

The inability to trust others, love others, or allowing yourself to be loved, are all symptoms of low self-esteem. These symptoms are from poor relationships, but they don't come from *your* poor relationships. They are not your fault and are not so obvious until *after* you have many failed relationships later on in life. It is only after coming to terms of what caused your failures is when you are able to forgive the source and make sure it does not happen to your offspring.

There are two ideas that one should consider when raising children that may not be so intuitive. The first one is that children should know that their parents have unconditional love for them. However, saying "I Love You" to a teenager has very little impact on them. What is more important is for them to know that you have their backs. It does not mean that you have to agree with them on every issue, it just means that children know that if they are ever stuck in a difficult situation, you will be there for them. This sets a strong baseline for positive self-esteem and independence throughout their lives.

The second most important thing when raising children is for the parent to understand what motivates each child. What works for one might not work for the other child. One of the worst things you can tell a child is "Why aren't you like your brother?" It's because they *are not* their brothers, they are unique and there is no one in the world like them. If your parents criticized you, or you were always compared to other children, that may be a source of your low self-esteem. If this is the case, you need to forgive your parents and understand that they did their best with the tools they were given. You can then make sure that *you* will not be the source for *your* children's low self-esteem.

Parents should not set impossibly high standards for their children, or themselves. This can lead to feelings of being inadequate when anyone is unable to meet those standards. This can be especially true with parents who have spent time and energy promoting the athletic careers of their children. This feeling of low self-esteem originates from aspirations that were never achieved, but it can even happen when they do succeed in athletics. Some athletes who have succeeded at the highest levels in their sport have had to struggle with low self-esteem. This includes athletes such as: the Williams sisters, Michelle Wie, Roy Jones, Jr, Andre Agassi, just to name a few.

Young adolescents who play sports should do it for the purpose of interacting with other children and having fun. Once a parent starts pushing a child to make it into his career, the pressure can be immense and can cause low self-esteem. Even if your child is going to grow to 6'9" in height, has great basketball skills, is extremely disciplined, it is still a long shot for them to be a successful professional basketball player. The parents should support it, but it should be in the context that the game is a way to make a living, not the way they should be defined as a person. That way if they don't succeed, which is the most likely scenario, they won't suffer with low-esteem. If the same child is only going to be 5'5" tall, one should never tell their child they will never succeed in basketball because of their height. This is something that a child will eventually figure out for themselves. Otherwise you telling your kid that they will never be tall enough to be in the NBA can be detrimental and possibly cause them to have low self-esteem.

Social interactions with peers and teachers can also influence a child's self-esteem. Positive feedback or validation from these interactions will boost their self-worth, while negative experiences or criticism can have the opposite effect. If you had critical teachers growing up, that might have been a contributing source of low self-esteem later on in life. Experiencing bullying or harassment can lead to feelings of shame, insecurity, and low self-worth. This is why parents need to be aware of their children's feelings and take action to protect them if needed.

Nothing boosts a child's or adult's self-esteem more than their achievements. Success in various areas of life, such as academics, sports, or hobbies, can contribute to a person's sense of self-worth. Hobbies are very helpful for positive feelings, even if a child does not stick with it. Trying to find a hobby that your child enjoys will help with improving low self-esteem. Parents should always support the hobbies of their children and give them encouragement at all times.

Then there are significant life events, such as trauma, abuse, or major life changes, which can have lasting effects on a person's self-esteem. There is a wide range of trauma and abuse and a certified therapist should be involved when children or adults are trying to recover from such past events.

While parents and caregivers may play a significant role in the development of a child's self-esteem, it is important to recognize that self-esteem is complex and multi-dimensional. One should be aware that there may be many influencing factors in someone's self-esteem throughout a person's life.

Why is understanding the source important to your self-esteem? Because once you can figure it out, you will know what steps to take to cure it. However, the most important thing is to forgive the source of your low self-esteem. Constantly blaming others for your challenges will just turn you into an injustice collector; that is not the kind of collector you want to be.

> *"Constantly blaming others for your challenges will just turn you into an injustice collector; that is not the kind of collector you want to be."*

It is much better to collect coins or stamps than to collect all the injustice that other people have done to you. This constant holding in of your emotional pain may never go away. Holding onto grudges, resentment, or negative feelings towards others can take a toll on your mental health. By practicing forgiveness, we release ourselves from the burden of carrying negative emotions and free ourselves to focus on all the positive aspects of life.

Parents also need to show resilience when they are in front of their children. That includes not blaming, complaining, and always trying to see the good in every situation. Life is always going to be throwing challenges our way, so you should not only be resilient, but act resilient in front of your children.

One example is how a parent deals with insects that invariably show up in everyone's house. They should never freak out or act scared when a spider, wasp, or mosquito makes a visit. They should act calm and do what it takes to get the bug out of the house, or into the toilet. A parent can use this example to teach compassion to their children by forcing a spider into a cup and tossing the insect outside. Parents that want to raise emotionally healthy children should not be the cause of those fears. Yes, wasps can sting, so you may have to kill it, but since most house spiders are harmless, the fear of spiders is irrational. Fear in one instance, can spread to other areas of life. Then you end up with grown children with foolish and unjustifiable fears.

There are many communities in America where they have a fear of dogs. Dogs were used to chase slaves who had escaped from their owners previous to their emancipation. Then there are the Nazis who used them to attack Jews in Europe during the second World War. Cynophobia is the overwhelming fear of dogs. People with this anxiety disorder feel intense fear and anxiety when they think about, see or encounter a dog. The excuse that most people use for this fear is that they had a negative experience with a dog when they were younger. Forgiving the source also means having the resilience to not let past fears control your life. Personally, I was bitten by my neighbor's German Shepard when I was about 4 or 5 years old. I did not let that affect me later on in life. In fact, I now own a dog and we use her to help other people get over their fear of dogs.

A teacher stands in front of her classroom with her arm stretched out holding a bottle of water in her palm. She asks the students how much the bottle of water weighs. The students give various answers from 6 ounces to 1 pound. She responds that the weight is meaningless. What is more important is that the longer she holds the bottle, the more pain she feels. If she holds it for a minute, there is no pain. If she holds it for an entire day, the pain will be excruciating. This is the same when we hold a grudge or don't forgive the source of our pain. The longer we hold it in, the more pain we feel.

Forgiving is a trait that happy people are able to do easily. Since you want to be one of those happy people, you will learn not to hold a grudge and live life with the ability to forgive. So learn to react to life's challenges with resilience and learn to forgive the source of your low self-esteem. You will find yourself being a much happier person.

2.
Be Happy With Internal Satisfaction

Not too long ago, we could get a deep sense of personal pleasure from a walk on a beach, watching a beautiful sunset, finishing a marathon, or seeing our children frolic in the park. Just the act of experiencing or accomplishing something was enough to make us feel good about ourselves, without the need for any external validation.

It was early in this century that when you traveled, you would bring your camera, or buy a disposable one from the drug store. After your vacation, you would take it to the drugstore or Costco and wait a week to get your pictures printed. Only then would you share it with your close friends and family, not your hundreds or thousands of Facebook or Instagram "friends."

These moments gave us self-satisfaction; happiness that comes from within us, not from anywhere or anyone else.

Social media has dulled this intrinsic reward. Rather than absorbing these moments for our own benefit, today, we share them with the world, seeking public affirmation of our lives. This quest for external validation pushes us to carefully stage moments for others to see.

If your satisfaction comes from others' approval, you will always need more of it. Yet people today experience more loneliness, anxiety and depression than at any point measured in history. So there must be something that is not working in this modern age of instant communication and social media.

This need of approval from others is similar when someone buys very expensive name brand clothing or handbags. If buying a Chanel or Louis Vuitton handbag would make you feel better about yourself for more than a few weeks, then therapists would be out of business. There are probably more therapists per capita in the world today than at any other time in history, yet our lives have never been more comfortable and convenient.

Truly confident individuals don't rely on showing off a Fendi or Hermes handbag, or have to name drop to feel secure in themselves. They find their self-worth from within and do not need external validations. Owning a designer handbag may bring momentary satisfaction, but it cannot replace the deep sense of self-assurance that comes from knowing, accepting, and loving oneself.

Body image can be a source of low self-esteem. This is especially true during adolescence and early adulthood, but it does not seem to end there. The recent phenomena of people showing off their bodies on social media plays such a major role in how you feel about yourself, no matter how old you are. We are bombarded with scenes of perfect bodies from everywhere you look: television/

internet ads, magazine covers and even video screens at malls and airports.

I have thought long and hard about body image and how much time we spend working out being laser focused on eating a vegan, vegetarian, Mediterranean, or plant based diet. I am a big fan of eating healthy because I believe you are what you eat. If you put junk in your body, you get junk out of your body. I believe we have become a society that is too focused on our body image. The reason why there are many advertisements for diets and workout gimmicks is because it influences people to buy their products!

What do you think is considered a healthy body shape in the images we see today bombarding our consciousness? The answer is a body that is thin, muscular, and tan. If you don't have that, you're out of shape, fat, and maybe even ugly. There does not appear to be any middle ground. I think these concepts are just the societal views and not the reality we should be living with.

When did having a tan become synonymous with healthy, good looks, while having pale skin was looked down upon? It's curious to observe how college students, particularly those from colder northern states, eagerly run outside on the first sunny spring day wearing bathing suits to catch a tan, even when the temperature barely reaches into the high 50's!

In movies that depict the 1800s early 1900s, affluent women were often portrayed as having fair, pale skin. The movie Titanic comes to mind as an example. They would stroll about with wide-brimmed hats and parasols shielding their faces from the sun. Being pasty white was considered beautiful. In contrast, having a tan was associated with the working class – those employed outside in the sun on farms or constructing railroads. Tanned skin was considered a marker of lower social standing, synonymous with poverty.

The narrative has shifted drastically over time. Today, being tan is often associated with being healthy and affluent, symbolizing a person who can afford to travel to sunny, exotic destinations. Whereas being pale means you have to work 80 hour weeks to afford rent and food and don't have any free time to be outside.

When did this shift in social perception occur? I would venture to guess that it coincided with the rise of the marketing industry, particularly when Madison Avenue transformed from just a street in Manhattan to a major epicenter of the marketing universe. The influence of Madison Avenue as a powerhouse in shaping public opinion likely played a pivotal role in redefining beauty standards and associating a tan with luxury and affluence.

At one time, being slightly overweight was considered sexy. Again, this is probably because if you were thin, you didn't eat because you could not afford to eat. However, in today's society, this is generally not an issue. So now carrying an extra 10-20 pounds can lead to feelings of inadequacy, potentially triggering negative emotions, which causes a person to eat more. This then becomes a vicious cycle and we end up 100 pounds overweight. More people die in America from the side effects of overeating than from starvation. We should stop this feeling that we are worthless if we are overweight. Once we realize that the source of our low self-esteem is being caused by whatever trends are influenced from the boardrooms of Madison Avenue, then we may be able to cure our low self-esteem.

Having a body that is healthy is something that everyone should strive for. However, being healthy is not indicated based on how tan or skinny one is. This has caused many in our society to be laser focused on the shape of individual body parts, or preoccupied with their weight. This focus on our bodies can be unhealthy and may play a major role in having low self-esteem. Once you understand the source of what is causing you to have low self-esteem, you will have an easier time being cured from it.

Your internal satisfaction starts with you knowing how awesome you really are and there are people that love you, even if you are struggling with loving yourself. Remember that happiness and contentment come from within and are not solely dependent on external circumstances or the opinions of others, no matter your: shape, size, skin color, clothes, purse, car, or even the likes on your social media. Learn to love and accept yourself as you are without the need for external validation and you'll find greater peace and fulfillment in life.

3.
Controlling Your Exposure, Emotional Vampires and Critical Thinking

Imagine that you had a garden blooming with stunning flowers. If you happen to notice that they were starting to wilt, would you blame the flowers? Would you call the seed manufacturer and complain about the seeds? It seems unlikely. More likely, you'd likely check the surroundings of the flower bed. You would make sure that they were receiving ample water, sunlight, and nutrient-rich soil.

We also thrive or wither emotionally based on our environment. Placing ourselves in the wrong environment lowers our self-esteem, preventing our inner light from shining. It's crucial to ensure that your surroundings contribute to your happiness and don't drag you down in life. Just as a flower needs the right conditions to bloom, we also need the right conditions to realize our fullest potential and share our brilliance with the world. This is why controlling your exposure is such an important element to your positive self-esteem.

You are the gatekeeper to your brain. It's crucial to keep out what makes you feel bad, and stay focused on what makes you happy. If any activity or interaction causes you to have low self-esteem, stay clear of it! This certainly includes people who bring you down. There is a reason that certain people are called downers, or what I like to call Emotional Vampires. While in theory, external factors, such as people, shouldn't affect your self-esteem; the reality is that they can.

Emotional Vampires are people who suck the energy out of you and cause you to be emotionally drained. Just like being aware of how you affect other people's self-esteem will help you to be more cognizant of your own, understanding people who drain you of energy will do the same thing. There are 5 categories of people or personality traits that may be causing this draining of your energy in your life. These may be people whose name you dread seeing in a text notification, on your calendar, or on a guest list. You may be in a relationship with them, they may be a co-worker, or most likely, a relative of yours.

Recognizing people who are emotional vampires will bring you clarity because who you hang out with is an important predictor of your emotional health. It does not mean you can't associate with the vampires, it just means that you need to find healthy boundaries.

5 Types of Emotional Vampires:

1. ***The victim:*** Loves to let people know how they're getting the short end of the stick in life. They often blame their misfortune on others and take no responsibility for their own actions. Everyone else is to blame and they will drag you down to their pessimistic level when you're with them.

2. ***The Narcissist:*** Narcissists only care about themselves and their own problems; they tend to take up all the oxygen in a room and need to be the center of attention. Typically, after you've spent time with a narcissist, you'll realize you barely got a word in, and they never asked you a single question about your life. They have a strong need to feed their desire for attention and admiration. They lack empathy for others and have an unrealistic view of their importance. They may be outwardly charming, but after some time with them, you find that they leave you drained.

3. ***The Drama Queen:*** They seek out and relish drama—you can easily spot these people in your social media feed, because they're always oversharing everything they experience, good or bad. They exaggerate beyond the norm to show what a horrible experience they had to go through.

4. ***The Socially Awkward:*** These are people who are difficult to be with because of their awkwardness. Usually, they are tolerable to be with when they are in a large group. Socializing one on one is difficult and draining. It is possible that this can be someone who is on the spectrum of having Aspergers. People who are aware that they have

a social disorder are usually easier to socialize with because they learn how to compensate for their deficiencies. It is the ones who are *not* aware of it that are difficult. Although they can't help it, knowing they have it will make you more tolerant and accepting.

5. ***Relatives, Spouses, or In-laws:*** Not only can they be one of the 4 categories above, if you were not related to them, you would have much more empathy towards them. Not all of our relatives are vampires, it's just that they have a different relationship with us than anyone else. You have no choice in that you have to interact with them, so that makes associating with them a little more volatile. It is possible that they are not emotional vampires with anyone else, except you. The example I like to use is when my 2 daughters were fighting over a pair of shoes. If they were best friends, there would've been no argument. You may be best friends with your mom if she was not your mom. It is just that the ones closest to us can cause us to be more sensitive and emotional.

Set boundaries with people that have to be in your life that are causing you low self-esteem. If they do not have to be in your life, consider avoiding them or at a minimum, take control of your exposure to them. Besides giving them a copy of this book, here are a few more ideas to control your exposure.

1. No one needs an all-access pass to your life.

2. You don't have to respond immediately to texts from those who need your attention.

3. Newly married couples may need to move away from parents or in-laws

You have the potential to be as happy as the people around you, so put yourself in the right environment to protect your happiness. This includes the people who you listen to on podcasts or the authors of the books you read. Surround yourself with inspiration, only engaging with material that uplifts and motivates you.

This is the same for any social media that you may be addicted to. If it is causing you negative emotions or impacting your mental-health, delete it! You will feel liberated and will feel a profound sense of freedom. I know many people who have deleted Facebook and Instagram and they could not be happier with the decision. Although it may be challenging, you may find yourself a significantly more joyful person.

If attending a social event, like a party, leaves you feeling uncomfortable or unhappy, it's important to prioritize your own well-being rather than succumbing to peer pressure from a friend who insists you go.

On a personal note, I receive many wedding invitations. Most of these weddings don't end into the early morning hours. As someone who values going bed early, staying past 10pm at a wedding makes me unhappy. I've communicated to my wife that eating a late dinner, which sometimes isn't served until after 11pm, isn't something I want to do, even only occasionally. Thankfully, she shares the sentiment, and together, we've decided that for future invitations, we'll attend the ceremony and skip the dinner and dancing.

This choice may not have crossed my mind in my 30s or 40s, but as I embrace my inner "cranky old man," prioritizing my happiness has taken precedence. It's a shift towards doing what brings joy and avoiding what detracts from it, a conscious decision to make my well-being a priority when it comes to social events.

In the past, when acquaintances on the street would suggest, "Hey, let's get together!" my default response was always a polite yes. However, now that I've gained more control over my self-esteem, you may hear this response: "No thank you." It's not necessarily about disliking the person; it could be that they're not a favorite of mine, but more likely it is just that I am just more intentional with my time. Every activity I engage in needs to serve a purpose, and if meeting with an acquaintance is just to schmooze, I may choose not to invest my time in it. Unlike those who can leisurely spend hours at a coffee house reading the newspaper, I'm not one of those people anymore. I've adopted a more purpose-driven approach to how I use my time, and that includes even while waiting in line at the grocery store.

Have you ever wondered why the gossip magazines that are by the checkout line in a grocery store rarely showcase blissful marriages? It seems that most headlines feature divorces and break-ups, especially when affairs, flings and large amounts of money are involved.

The truth is, editors of magazines and entertainment shows understand that dysfunctional relationships tend to capture more attention than healthy ones. Unfortunately, the media thrives on bad news because it sells. So they just overlook the heartwarming stories of couples deeply in love for decades. Those are exactly the kinds of relationships we should be reading about and emulating. Constant exposure to this kind of dysfunction can erode your self-esteem, so it's wise to consider reducing your consumption of news about the gossip of other people's lives.

Let's get back again to the purpose of the marketing executives on Madison Avenue. Their job is to think about ways to make you feel bad about yourself so that you will buy the product they are selling. Their job is to try to find that emotional selling point, or what is referred to as ESP. This is where you feel like you are not happy unless you own their product. For sure, it is exciting when you see the latest car commercial, or see young men drinking Modelo Especial beer with stunning models hanging on their arms. That excitement is rooted from our own insecurities as we subconsciously believe that acquiring these products, or even these models, will lead to a better life.

This can lead us to having low self-esteem for two reasons. If we are not able to spend the money on what they are selling, then we feel inadequate because we are not wealthy enough to have it. If we can afford to buy what they are selling, then we might buy the product, and then regret it later because that quick burst of endorphins that we received for the first few days of owning it eventually disappeared. This can lead to post-purchase regret as we question the reason behind spending money on something that, in retrospect, didn't bring the lasting satisfaction we anticipated.

Have you ever observed the products sold on cruise ships, or the first stores you see at ports where cruise ships dock, or those nearest to casinos in places like Las Vegas? They often feature jewelry and art. I can't be the only one to go on vacation in Mexico and buy a souvenir like a sombrero, only to later question why I acquired something I really have no use for? This happens because, during travel, we are usually in a positive emotional state, influenced by the excitement of being in new surroundings.

When your emotions are high, you are more likely to use your credit card. Art and jewelry most likely will have the highest markup of any product you can buy. Sometimes it can be ten times the wholesale cost, especially for something that is a one-of-a-kind. With one-of-a kind items, there is no way for you to compare pricing.

Marketing executives know how our mind works and that's why they know where to place these products, where your emotions are highest. I have a rule that I don't buy any tchotchke (Yiddish for a small, decorative item or souvenir, usually of no particular value) when I am traveling. You might say to yourself, "but I really do like the Italian Murano glass I bought in Venice, Italy." That's true, you still like it, or pretend to say you still like it because you don't want to admit it was an emotional purchase. No one likes to admit they made a mistake, so they cover up their regret with, "I still like it."

After your kids break some of them, and then you break some of them while cleaning off the dust, eventually that excitement wears off and you might come to admit that those vacation purchases weren't so wise. If this does not happen in a few years after the purchase, it certainly will happen when you try to downsize and sell your house. Then you'll come to accept that most of these purchases were for nothing when your garage is full of junk that you have no use for. Understanding that you are emotionally happier when traveling and will more likely spend money on things you don't need will help you to be aware and in more control of your self-esteem. The only sombrero you should ever buy is the upside down one made into a pottery dish for chips and salsa. At least that one you'll use more than once in your life.

Exercising critical thinking is also a good idea when consuming news. You must understand the source, its context, and the motives of the one reporting it. Media outlets carry biases that shape their reporting, whether intentional or not, which can influence how they report. This became particularly evident during the 2020 pandemic.

There was probably lots of low self-esteem caused from the constant blaring of news about masks and vaccines.

Whether it was the severity of the disease or the effectiveness of certain measures, like lockdowns and school closings, it was enough to give you anxiety. You should have the attitude that anything you hear, especially from a news source, is sensationalized in one way or the other. Positive reports may not be as optimistic as portrayed, and negative events might not be as dire as they seem. Remember that the media's primary aim is to capture and retain your attention.

Critical thinking is a necessary skill to develop in today's information-saturated world. If you're not critically thinking, you put yourself at risk to develop low self-esteem. Build a fence around your happiness, and exercise control over your exposure by removing anything that diminishes your self-esteem. I know it may be hard, but it's also hard on your emotional state to feel bad about yourself. In the end, both choices are hard, so choose the hard that gets you to where you are happy with yourself. Or else you'll end up hosting parties with emotional vampires sucking the energy out of you while serving them chips and salsa in ceramic sombreros.

4.
Discovering and Living With Your Core Values

Do you know what your core values are? Can you list them if you were asked? There is one reason why your core values are important in helping improve your self-esteem. If you don't know what they are, when it comes to making a choice in life, your decisions may be influenced by someone else's values, not your own.

Core values are an individual, or even an organizations', fundamental beliefs that drive their behavior, actions and decision making. They are considered an essential part of one's identity. They help a person prioritize their goals and purpose in life. Defining your core values will help you to avoid any low self-esteem. If you don't know what they are, you may be struggling in life.

It is very similar to what someone perceives as success in life. If you don't define it yourself, someone else will probably end up doing it for you. You might go through life without having any idea what success is, and then you may blow right by it without realizing it. You may then go through a midlife crisis because you had no clarity about what success is and missed it. Maybe what you thought your definition of success is actually someone else's definition. The same is true regarding your core values.

I have thought a lot about my core values in life and what guides me. If you had asked me in my twenties, I might not have known what they were. The more I have lived life, the more I know what is important to me, and what is not important to me. I understand your values may not be so clear when you are younger. You just have not lived long enough to see the outcome of your actions. There is an idea that you don't really have wisdom until you are fifty years old. I can say that there is some truth to that.

The following are a list of some of the core values I have acquired throughout the years. Many of the following I have discovered through my writings and classes I teach. These are what I call nuggets of wisdom. It is good to have these mantras in your brain so you can recall them when needed. Some of them are:

- Think before you speak.
- Use your speech for peace, not conflict.
- Live in clarity, not contradiction.
- Always complement, never criticize.
- The journey of life is the endgame.
- For every good thing that happens to you, something bad will come out of it. For anything bad that happens to you, something good will come out of it.

- Thank God for all the good in your life, as well as the bad.
- Life is not about getting things, but becoming someone.
- The greatest transformation you will make in your life is when you believe in yourself as much as God believes in you.
- We are human beings, not human doings.
- Your ego is not your amigo.
- You can never negotiate with someone when they are emotional.
- Live for your soul and you will end up with the body that your ego is happy with.
- The two happiest days of a boat owner are the day he buys the boat, and the day he sells the boat.
- It's your job to change the world, not let the world change you.

If you are not sure of what your values are, the easiest way is to start off with finding someone you admire for their positive characteristics and qualities. This can be your grandmother, a teacher, or a social media person that you follow. Make a list of what it is that you admire about them. That can be a good starting point. Chances that words like, disciplined, kind, and selfless may come into your vernacular.

If you are having trouble coming up with your core values, here are some other ways to help you define them:

What brings you joy in life? List the values that are needed to achieve that joy. For example, if you appreciate how celebrities are admired and respected, that means you want to feel like you are admired and respected for who you are. Your value should be to pursue endeavors that earn the respect and admiration of others. This includes how you treat other people, because people will treat you like you treat them.

Have you gone through a situation that made you feel uncomfortable or conflicted? List the values needed so you won't fall into the same situation. Maybe you were involved in a business and feel that you were cheated. It is possible that there was no clear communication of the roles and responsibilities that each of you played in the deal. Maybe your core value should be anticipating situations that can come up in a business deal and making sure that you have answers to any problems that may arise.

Are there some values that are non-negotiable? What are some things that would make you cringe if you saw someone else do them? Have you ever been in a shopping mall and saw a mother berate her children? If that makes you uncomfortable, maybe controlling your anger is one of your core values.

Is there something you would be willing to die for?

General Patton told his troops before he sent them into battle with the Nazi's, "You think your job is to die for your country? Your job is not to die for your country. Your job is to get the other guy to die for his."

Instead of dying for the things you believe in, live for the things you believe in. Prioritize the most important things in your life. If you have children, maybe your core value would be family first.

Are you living in contradiction with your values? Do you talk a big game, but don't actually hold by what you preach?

> *Imagine if I asked a classroom full of people if they did any acts of kindness to anyone in the past 3 days. I would venture to guess that an entire room full of hands would go up. Then if I asked the class something specific that they acted kind upon, I would get a bunch of blank stares. I would then tell the class maybe they only do acts of kindness in theory, but when it comes to the act itself, they might have fallen short.*

Maybe you never want to be overweight, so maybe not overeating, or only eating until you are half full is a core value of yours. We may talk or think about our values, but are we really sticking to them? If you want to be a healthy person, are you doing healthful things in your life?

What values do you want to be known for? Start with the end game in mind and think about what you want people to say at your eulogy. This is a great way to live the life that you really want.

Be willing to reevaluate your values as you gain wisdom in life. Make an effort to align your actions and decisions with your values. We all do things when we are young that we cringe about when we are older. It is okay for your core values to change as you mature.

Learn to say no to opportunities or commitments that don't align with your values. Saying no is an empowering act that allows you to prioritize what is truly important to you.

Defining your core values is an ongoing journey of discovering who you really want to be. Defining your core values, even if you can't always live by them, will help you to have strong self-esteem, because you know where you want to be in life, even if you are not there yet.

5.
List of Attributes

Have you ever taken a moment to reflect on the remarkable attributes you possess? Consider these functions you have when you wake up that you probably take for granted: the ability to walk to the bathroom, all the holes in your body working correctly, the gift of sight, and the ability to hear the morning birds chirp. These are some of the greatest gifts bestowed upon you. It often takes you losing them to really appreciate them when we suffer challenges to our health. To experience genuine happiness, make a list of all the things you have that money can't buy.

> *"To experience genuine happiness, make a list of all the things you have that money can't buy"*

To elevate your self-esteem, consider visiting a children's hospital or an old age home. Such experiences have a profound way of building appreciation for one's own circumstances. It's when we encounter individuals facing poverty, destitution, illness, or physical limitations like being confined to a wheelchair, that we gain a heightened perspective on our own place in life, prompting a sense of gratitude and self-worth.

> *"Picture a scene at a stoplight on Wilshire Blvd, where a man in his older looking Honda comes to a halt at the stoplight. In the adjacent lane, a sleek BMW pulls up, catching his eye. The Honda driver can't help but think, 'I dream of the day when I can afford a car like that.'*
>
> *Right beside the Honda, an aging Chrysler, showing signs of rust and dings, comes to a creaking stop. The Chrysler's driver gazes at the Honda and wishes that someday I will be able to own a reliable vehicle like that.*
>
> *Then a cyclist rolls up to the same intersection. As he pedals to a stop, he thinks to himself, 'One day, I hope to own a clunker, so I won't have to bike to work'*
>
> *And then, a pedestrian waiting for the light to change says to himself, 'I can't wait for the day when I have a bicycle of my own to ride to school.'*
>
> *Finally, as the traffic light is counting down, a man in a wheelchair watches the world go by. He whispers to himself, 'I wish for nothing more than to have my legs back so I can walk on my own.'»*

The moral to this story is that we always think we will be happier with something more than we have, when in reality, we should be happy with what we possess. What we have would bring joy to many people. Being aware of your list of attributes can be a powerful tool to help you live with gratitude. When you have the attitude of gratitude toward life's experiences, you can begin the journey towards healing low self-esteem. If your life is based on comparison, you will always fall short. Make a list of your attributes and embrace a life of gratitude. You will never have to worry about having low self-esteem ever again.

6.
Rejection Therapy

The more you get used to facing rejection, regardless of the circumstances, the more your self-esteem can soar. It may seem paradoxical, but consider this; professions like door-to-door salespeople often showcase remarkable self-esteem. Despite encountering many closed doors, they persist, recognizing that each rejection brings them closer to a successful sale.

I came across the teachings of Wayne Hoffman, a globally renowned mentalist, who emphasizes the crucial lesson that achieving more 'yeses' in life often involves encountering more 'nos.' In one of his demonstrations, Hoffman invited an audience volunteer to join him at the front. Equipped with a two-sided yes/no coin, he proposed a deal; the volunteer had thirty seconds to make as many flips as possible, earning $20 for each 'yes' and facing no repercussions for landing on 'no.' With enthusiasm, the volunteer engaged in the coin-flipping challenge, securing seven 'yes' responses alongside an almost equal number of 'nos.' Hoffman promptly rewarded their efforts with $140 in cash. The insightful lesson emerged: the quantity of 'yeses' outweighs the significance of 'nos,' and taking more chances increases the likelihood of encountering both. While facing rejection is a common aspect of our pursuits, the potential negative consequences are typically minimal, involving brief discomfort or embarrassment. Conversely, a 'yes' often leads to positive outcomes on various fronts. This is precisely why Hoffman ensured there was no financial loss or penalty for flipping a 'no.'

In a real-world example, without the same level of clarity, the individual would likely have overthought the situation and might not have taken action. This is counterproductive; if you take more chances, the ratio of 'yeses' to 'nos' may not change. While you'll get a lot of 'nos,' you will get more 'yeses.' If you see a person who appears to have received a lot of 'yeses,' you can be sure they've also been rejected many times as well. A critical element in getting more of what we seek is enduring plenty of rejections along the way.[6]

Just to be clear, flipping a no in a coin toss is not the same feeling of rejection that you would get if you got turned down for a job, or dumped by your boyfriend, but it is this precise way of thinking that will help you to build yourself up into the person that does not fear rejection. In fact, you may even learn to thrive on it!

Engaging in rejection therapy is a powerful tool for cultivating confidence and boosting self-esteem. An effective way to practice this is by making a habit of saying hello to every person you pass on the street. While it might seem a bit strange, this simple act serves as a valuable exercise to strengthen your ability to handle rejection. The idea is

---

[6] Robert Glazers' *Friday Forward* weekly email

that the more you experience rejection, even in seemingly trivial situations like greeting strangers on the street, the more resilient you become. This newfound resilience can significantly ease the process of facing rejection in more significant areas of life, such as job applications or asking someone out on a date.

When I have the desire to say hello to everyone I pass on the street, I seize the opportunity and do it. Every interaction is a chance to build my confidence and self-esteem. I will even vary how I greet people: Hey, How's it goin', Hi, Hellooooo, Hey, I like your shirt! (Hat, shoes, or whatever else is sticking out like a sore thumb.) Sometimes I will even change my voice to make it sound slightly funny.

When I was in my early twenties, I used to have a hard time getting a date. My friend Barry taught me that I have to look at dating just as a batter faces down a pitcher in baseball. If you don't swing at the ball, you will never hit a home run. I know it seems like a simple concept, but this little analogy gave me so much more confidence! The legacies of such players as Bryce Harper and Babe Ruth are not made from remembering them for their strike outs, but for how many home runs they hit. So look at striking out as part of the overall picture, not what you will be remembered for, and you won't be afraid to swing at the ball.

Once you start to get desensitized to being rejected, then your self-esteem will start to build. Here are a few other ideas that you can use to help you:

- Be overly nice to sales people or waiters. Try to strike up a conversation by asking them where they are from or if they like their job.
- Offer to buy the person who is next to you in the Starbucks or Dunkin' Doughnuts line a coffee.

This will really make your day and theirs as well. You may even strike up a conversation with them. It's only a few bucks and is much cheaper than going to a therapist!

- When you get to your seat on a plane, immediately say hello to the person who is sitting next to you. Although you don't have to say anything else, you just took out any awkwardness that there might have been.

I was on a recent flight from Pittsburgh to New York and during the train ride to the gates, I noticed a person from a different background than mine, possibly a Muslim. He seemed to take an interest in me, possibly because I was wearing a Kippa (a skullcap or Yarmulke). At one point, our eyes met, and I couldn't help but notice that they were giving me an intense glare, kind of like he wanted to kill me.

Now, in the past I might have been nervous or scared, but I just smiled and thought about what this poor guy must be going through. Here is just a guy going to work in a restaurant at the airport, and then he sees me, and then allows himself to have this anger build up inside of him. I started to feel bad for him that he has to go through life not being able to control his emotions. After about 10 seconds of being concerned, I did not let it bother me anymore and went on with my day. It is because I have allowed myself to get rejected enough times, that I won't let someone else's issues ruin my self-esteem, or even my day.

Rejection therapy really does work and it will make you a much happier person, with a higher level of self-esteem. So go out and get rejected!

7.
Familiar and Comfortable Are Not The Same

Have you ever noticed how the price of a bottle of water can vary depending on where you buy it? In a typical grocery store, you may expect to pay around $1 for a bottle. At the gym, that price may jump to $2. Head to a convention center, and you're likely looking at $3 for the same bottle. And if you attend a concert or a sports event, be prepared to shell out $4, or even $5.

Now, you may wonder; what justifies these varying prices for a simple bottle of water? The truth is, the actual product doesn't change at all; it's the same water. The difference in cost is entirely based on the location and the context.

Grocery stores generally offer competitive prices, striving to stay on par with their nearby competitors. This means you'd feel taken advantage of if they charged you $5 for that bottle of water. In contrast, at a concert or sports venue, you may grumble about the price, but the convenience and experience factor in. People are often willing to pay more in these settings, which can make the $30 you shell out for a hot dog, french fries, and beer seem more palatable.

So, the next time you contemplate the cost of that bottle of water, remember that it's not about the water itself, but where you are and the value you place on the convenience at the moment.

To bolster your self-esteem and cultivate your sense of self-worth, you may need to get out of a familiar place that does not place a high value on you. Familiarity is a nice thing, but only if you are truly happy where you are. That familiar place may give you a sense of security, but it may be placing a low value on you. You may have bought into that perception and it is keeping you from thriving. Much like the value of the bottle of water depends on your location, your self-worth can be heavily influenced by your surroundings. Here are some compelling reasons why breaking away from the familiar can be immensely beneficial:

- Exploring different environments and leaving what you are familiar with can be an eye-opening experience. It can help you appreciate, or not appreciate, the value of the place you are familiar with and whether it truly aligns with your best interests. Often, it's easy to take for granted what we have until it's no longer there.

- You might have been in an unhealthy environment, mistakenly associating it with comfort merely because it was familiar. It's crucial to recognize that familiarity and comfort are not always synonymous. While something familiar can be comforting, being comfortable doesn't always necessitate familiarity. Being in a familiar place doesn't automatically mean it's the right place for you. Breaking away from the familiar and embracing potentially comforting, but unfamiliar situations can significantly boost your self-esteem.

- Sometimes, you may find yourself in a toxic relationship. Even if it feels familiar, it takes stepping out of it to realize how detrimental it was for your well-being. What you once considered comforting may in reality have been nothing more than a familiar pattern, and not only is it not comforting, but harmful for you.

- Being in a new, unfamiliar environment could also introduce you to people who prioritize personal growth, ultimately aiding you in reaching your full potential.

Embracing new experiences will allow you to open up in ways that being in the same old place will never achieve. It is kind of like a cactus that is sitting on your windowsill in Manhattan. It never surpasses more than 5 or 6 inches in height. Yet, when you take that same cactus and plant it in the desert of Arizona, it can flourish and grow to be 10 feet tall, or more! This disparity exists because the windowsill in New York City is not the right environment for a cactus. It needs to be where it can thrive. It is possible that where you are in your life, you are stunting your growth and you're limiting the heights of your self-esteem.

Stepping out of familiar situations increases your confidence and you will have a more secure sense of who you are as a person. I see this all the time where I teach in Jerusalem. Students from diverse backgrounds come from all over the world to absorb wisdom. These students quickly figured out that being in their usual familiar environment was a handicap. When they get away from their familiar environment with their families, which they originally thought was comfortable, they display a remarkable willingness to learn and grow. They find that their new environment aligns more with their ideals and aspirations. After a few days of classes, many of these students have gone against their parents wishes and stayed longer than they intended.

I used to hold scotch and sushi events in my house when I lived in Maryland. It consisted of about 30 minutes of schmoozing, followed by a 30-minute class on Jewish spirituality that incorporated a strong focus on personal growth. I would normally invite about 50 people, but usually only between 8-12 would show up. The people that showed up really enjoyed my classes. The topics seemed to open up their minds because the discussions would sometimes go on for hours! When I do a similar event in Jerusalem, I can only invite about 10 people. It's not the difference in the size of the space that I have to consider between the two cities, it's the amount of people that show up. If I invited 50 people in Jerusalem, 150 people would show up! It would be a complete opposite turnout from having the event in Maryland.

This is why getting out of familiar environments can help you improve your low self-esteem, whether or not they are comfortable. This is how you improve your resilience. Resilience is the capacity to withstand or to recover quickly from difficulties.

I personally believe that lack of resilience is the reason for so much depression and low self-esteem. This lack of resilience probably stems from too much comfort in our life. Life is too easy. Everything is available to us at all times. We are living in the best time in the history of the world. Although many believe that our children will *not* be as well off as this current generation, it may only be that way as far as financial wealth. With the massive increase in technology and efficiencies in all parts of our lives, our children may be less wealthy, but they won't need as much money to get the same benefits as we have now.

You could write many books on the advancements that we have in our lives today compared to just 50 years ago. One of the most incredible advancements has been the availability of information and consumer goods. Have the advancements made us any happier as individuals? If you are reading this book, then probably not. It was not that long ago that if you ordered something by mail, it would take a few weeks. Now with same day delivery, there is nothing that we can't get, almost instantly. Who would have ever thought that you could have a personal computer in your pocket that would have access to all the information in the world. The phones we have in our pockets now are more powerful than any of the Apollo spacecraft that went to the moon.

The iPhones 6 can perform instructions 120 million times faster than the best Apollo Spacecraft computers. You wouldn't be wrong in saying an iPhone could be used to guide 120 million Apollo-era spacecraft to the moon, all at the same time.

You would think that all this access to affordable lightning fast information, instant communication, food, and consumer goods would make us the happiest generation ever. The poorest people today in America have comforts that the most wealthy people from 100 years ago could never have imagined. If we are so comfortable, why are we so miserable?

In Rabbi Stephen Baars' book, Win, he writes about how when we look back at our lives, sometimes the most meaningful times were when we were in the most uncomfortable time of our life.7 The reason for this is because besides resilience, living with a purpose brings meaning into our lives. Having meaning and purpose are the most valuable ways to live with strong self-esteem. Purpose being forward looking, and meaning is something you look back on. When you have a purpose in life, that creates meaning. Both of these will also help increase resilience in a person's mentality. While building resilience will help you get through difficult situations, as you will read about in the next excerpt, you will find yourself not having to deal with low self-esteem later in life.

"When you have a purpose in life, that creates meaning"

Excerpt from Win:

"Let me take you back to my high school, an all-boys' facility in London.

My teachers' generation saw the First World War and reveled in the glow, albeit dimming, British Empire.

And yet, relative to the life my teacher had growing up, it was we, the new generation that were really living the dream life. It was a new age in everything. The quality of life was unmatched in the history of humanity. Technology, health and wealth were so much greater than anything

---

[7] Wellstone Press

previous. And so it annoyed me to no end when people of that generation would tell us that it was they who really had it good!

Why did it irk me so?

Because there was nothing that I could find in that history to justify such fond reminisces. As such, I concluded a strange truth. My English teacher must be right. Why?

Because no matter who I asked, whatever their age, their pasts were always the good old days. This led me to a most paradoxical conclusion, that one day in my future I too will look back at this present as the "good old days."

The time that many of them were referring to as their good old days was The Blitz of London! Which, by all accounts, were some of the darkest days of Europe. In pure quality of life, their latter days were much better than their former.

So how could their past be the good old days, and not their present?

It took me four decades to figure it out, but this will explain it. Youth places a high value on the future. That mechanism can make any time great, no matter how bad it really is. It's like the day your parents announce you're going to Disneyland, the day you got engaged, the day you win the lottery. That day, because it's full of expectation of a great future, makes it phenomenal – no matter what condition your day is in now.

That teacher had fond memories of his youth, because at that time he looked forward to his future. And even though those earlier days were really terrible, and his latter days great, it makes no difference – it's his youth that he misses.

Plus, when he finally got to that anticipated future, there was now little to look forward to. Thus, by default, the older people get, the less they enjoy their present. Even though this, the present, is the tomorrow they were always looking forward to!

I know this is complicated, but it is really key to your success, so please excuse me as I try to re-state it another way so that it will be clear.

It's 1945, you weigh 75 pounds, every single member of your family is dead or murdered. You own nothing, literally, except the ragged shirt on your back. However, news reaches you that your camp, Auschwitz, has been liberated and the Allies have won the war. Forevermore, that day will be the best day of your life. Not the day you land in America, not the day you marry, not the day you have your first child, and not the day you make your first million dollars! These events pale compared to that day in 1945. For this simple reason, on that day the future was glowing blazing bright. No matter how good, or how bad your day is, it's the future that makes your day.

Those who were children in London during World War II worked very hard at making their future lives better, and by all accounts they succeeded gloriously. We live in the world that they created, and it's far better than the world they were born into. Yet, it's their youth that they miss!

Do you realize what happened here? They didn't end up enjoying life more, even though their lives were better.

You too, are not going to enjoy the world you are desperately trying to create, as much as the life you have now!

I have nothing against improving people's living conditions. It's a lovely thing to enjoy life, but increasing the quality of your life does not necessarily equate to an equal amount of enthusiasm for that life. If anything, and much to many people's chagrin, it's an inverse relationship.

As we mentioned above, the Holocaust survivor has an incredible day on the day he was liberated, simply because he foresees a great future. But as he inches closer towards that future he proportionately loses his excitement. People engage in the most futile attempts at avoiding this rule. Denial can keep you going for a long time, and substance abuse can stretch it out a little longer, but eventually everyone over the age of approximately 35 will have to face, in some form of awareness or another, that they enjoyed life a lot more when they were kids.

Don't mistake my words, few of us want to go back to living as we did, and even if we could, that is not the solution. Even the Holocaust survivor will agree to that.

It's not the things that we had then that we miss, it's the things we expected to have that gave us our excitement. This is what we are missing now.

Trading your mini-van for a red Ferrari is not going to have any greater impact on your life than when you got your mini-van in the first place. It's not a change in your outer world that is in need, but the inner one.

Think back to when you were six years old, the idea that tomorrow you were going to Disneyland made tomorrow an incalculably high number. At whatever age you are now, going to Disneyland is no longer going to have that same impact. Why?

Because you've been to Disneyland, and the fantasy is rarely as exciting as the real thing.

> *As a student told me when he got his first Porsche, "Owning one is nice, but the anticipation was better." You just can't replay that movie again and enjoy it the same way. Once you've tasted it and realized it isn't that great, then you cannot recreate that anticipation. And it's the anticipation that gives life its excitement and thrill.*
>
> *Simply put, there is nothing you can do today to make today great. To make today great you need a phenomenal tomorrow."*

So how do you make tomorrow phenomenal? Plan for something that you are not familiar with or maybe not that comfortable doing. Embrace new experiences that you may have otherwise have never done.

- Go to a movie by yourself(Theaters are usually empty in the late morning when they start showing films).
- Hike to an area that you have never been to before.
- Go to lunch by yourself at a restaurant that you may have never considered going to.
- Take public transportation to a mall or museum you have never been to.
- Write a blog or an article about something you are passionate about.
- Go to an unfamiliar cafe to write your article.
- Take a class you may have never considered before.
- Go to a concert, especially one where you can sing along.

Familiarity is comforting, but comforting does not have to be familiar. Although getting out of your comfort zone will help you cure your low self-esteem, the irony lies in the fact that this act itself becomes familiar over time, promoting the need for continuous exploration. Then you will be in this endless loop of having to get away from what is familiar and do it all over again!

Exploring new avenues of learning is a proven strategy to enhance your self-esteem. Consider individuals who consistently enroll in classes and pursue additional educational degrees throughout their lives. These individuals often possess robust self-esteem because they actively seek opportunities for personal development and growth. Embracing a continuous learning mindset not only expands your knowledge, but also instills a sense of accomplishment and confidence, contributing to a positive self-image.

As you consistently pursue activities that bring you joy, each moment contributes to the creation of a phenomenal tomorrow. In essence, your continuous journey becomes the ultimate destination, and this approach is key to maintaining a high level of positive self-esteem throughout your life.

8.
Set a New Goal For Yourself

Setting new goals can be a powerful tool to combat low self-esteem. However, it's essential to acknowledge that simply setting goals without a plan can lead to disappointment. It's crucial to have set meaningful and achievable goals while having a well-thought-out system in place. Keep in mind that the primary aim is not just achieving these goals, but to also boost your self-esteem and confidence.

We'll explore two effective methods for goal-setting, aiming to redirect your focus away from your low self-esteem. As you progress on this journey, you'll gradually find that you've reduced those negative feelings about yourself. This transformation happens because you're dedicated to achieving something new and challenging. It's a fantastic way to boost your self-esteem and feel great about yourself!

A SMART goal the is a well-defined and structured goal-setting framework that stands for **S**pecific, **M**easurable, **A**chievable, **R**elevant, and **T**ime-bound.[8] Using the SMART criteria helps ensure that your goals are clear, attainable, and actionable. Here's what each component of a SMART goal means:

Specific: Your goal should be clear and specific, leaving no room for ambiguity. It should answer the questions: What do you want to accomplish? Why is it important? Who is involved and where will it happen?

Measurable: You need to have a way to track your progress and determine when you've achieved your goal. Ask yourself: How will you measure your success? What are specific benchmarks that you can use?

Achievable: Your goal should be realistic and attainable within the limits of your resources and abilities. You need to be real with yourself and ask if you can realistically achieve this goal. Do you have what I call the 3 D's of success? And it's not Don't Dilly Dally. It comprises of Desire, Determination, and Discipline. Desire is what I am trying to achieve. Determination is never quitting, and discipline is being regimented.

Relevant: Your goal should align with your core values and be relevant to your life or work. Ask yourself if this goal is worthwhile and is it the best time of your life to achieve it. For example, if you plan to get married one day, there are some goals that become irrelevant to your life once you have a spouse.

Time-bound: You need to set a deadline for your goal. This creates a sense of urgency and helps you stay focused. Ask yourself: What is the target date for achieving this goal?

---

[8] A term first proposed by George T. Doran in the November 1981 issue of Management Review

Getting in shape by the end of the year is not a SMART goal because it lacks specificity and measurable criteria. "Running a 10k race is indeed a SMART goal because it meets all the components of the SMART framework.

While setting a goal to write a book by the end of the year can be a feasible target for experienced authors, it may be more advisable for first-time authors to start with smaller steps, like composing an article or blog post. These accomplishments can provide experience and build confidence, making the ultimate goal of writing a book more attainable, especially for those new to the writing process.

Setting a goal that you want to be married by the end of the year may be specific, but that does not mean it is realistic. Having a baby by a certain date may fit all the characteristics of a *SMART* goal, except it may not be attainable. These are all fantastic goals, but the problem is if it does not fulfill all the characteristics of a SMART goal, then you may be setting yourself up for a letdown, which will not be a positive development for your self-esteem.

If you have problems getting to your goals, start with a very easy goal that you know you can achieve. "Every morning, I will clean my room, make my bed, and hang my towel up." If you can't do this, then you have more serious problems than this book can solve.

Making your goal smart will help you with your low self-esteem. Does that mean you will always achieve your goals? Not at all, but that does not mean you still won't achieve something *more* than if you didn't set goals.

My personal example is that I had decided I was going to train for a marathon. I did not set that goal for myself based on the fact that I really wanted to run a marathon. I did it based on past experiences that when I used to run, I had increased creativity in my writing and was a more engaging speaker.

Setting a *smart* goal can be a tremendous help in your life. So here is another way on how to help you to set a new goal for yourself.

5 Steps to Successful Goal-Setting

First, write 10 of the most important goals that you want to accomplish. Then take out your pretend magic wand and pick the one that you would want to have in 24 hours. Let's make the assumption that this is the one that will have the greatest impact on your life! Now circle it. Now the 5 steps:

- Write that one goal on a clean sheet of paper.
- Set a deadline.
- Write down everything you have to do to achieve that goal. This includes breaking your goals down into easier bite size pieces.
- Organize it into a priority checklist.
- Take action *almost* everyday.

I don't strongly advocate the idea of sticking to a daily routine for certain specific activities. Many experts insist that writers should write every day, I find this approach unrealistic because there are days when time constraints make it impossible. When you inevitably miss a day, the self-imposed pressure can lead to self-criticism, potentially discouraging you from writing altogether.

I view writing, or any goal-setting pursuit, as a fluctuating trend. Some days, creativity flows effortlessly, while on others, motivation may be lacking. I prefer focusing on writing during those moments when inspiration strikes and abstaining when it doesn't. This flexibility allows for a more sustainable and enjoyable writing experience.

This is similar to when exercise is part of achieving your goal. Something is always better than nothing. If you are going to run 3 miles a day, but one day you do not have the time, run just 1/2 mile! Or don't run at all and call it your rest day. Rest days are helpful in enabling you to have a better run the next day that you do run.

Setting goals for yourself will help you to improve your low self-esteem, even if you don't achieve them. But at a minimum, make sure your goals are ***SMART***.

9.
Make Life Fun

Life should be fun! If it isn't, then you need to change how you view everything from the simplest tasks of putting on your shoes to preparing dinner. The same is true when it comes to the topic of love. If you think of love as a game that you like to play, like Scrabble, then you will play it! But if love becomes a joyless endeavor, then you won't play it. This is how you should live your life. You will generally like to do things that you love, and therefore your life will then be an enjoyable one, without having to manage with any low self-esteem. So strive to infuse joy into your everyday activities and goals and you will avoid having to deal with low self-esteem.

No one forced Mozart to study chemistry and Steve Jobs probably wasn't passionate about grammar. Tom Brady probably didn't dedicate his week to piano lessons. They pursued their paths because they not only found joy in what they did, but also because it's fun for them.

The concept I'm sharing with you was inspired by my experience with Montessori schools while raising my children. The Montessori philosophy centers on allowing children to learn in their own unique ways. It emphasizes the importance of granting children the freedom to select the subjects they wish to explore within the classroom. In Montessori, all projects are hands-on and interactive, fostering a different approach compared to conventional elementary schools.

In traditional elementary schools, teachers typically dictate the daily lesson plans, leaving little room for individual choice. Not every student is equally enthused about subjects like math, social studies, or science. Consequently, some children may struggle to engage with the material and may resort to daydreaming, slacking off, or worse, misbehaving.

The key takeaway is that what works for the majority of students may not necessarily be optimal for each individual. Montessori education focuses on a personalized learning experience that accommodates each child's unique interests and strengths.

The thought of being a brain surgeon probably does not sound fun for most people. However, for the students that have the memory of learning being fun, they won't focus on the grueling effort to become a brain surgeon! Imagine how much more you can accomplish when everything becomes fun!

As I am writing this, I am flying at 40,000 feet somewhere over the vast expanse of the Atlantic Ocean. Many people do not enjoy flying, but they do it because they have to. I actually enjoy getting on an airplane. I like to make everything fun, so I made flying fun. I look at the fact that I am sitting in an aluminum tube at 40,000 feet above the earth, moving at 600 MPH, all the while a flight attendant brings me a hot meal and soda or hot coffee. This is also one of the few places that I can write uninterrupted.

Where else can I find a situation like that? I don't even care about how good or bad the food is because I look at it as an experience, not a gourmet meal. So even though I am sitting in coach class, it can still feel like first class if you have the right attitude. It was not many years ago that if you wanted to go to Europe, you had to take a boat. Flying commercial airlines is somewhat of a recent phenomena, so we should really be grateful and not take it for granted. To make flying fun, have the attitude of gratitude at altitude. So I've managed to make flying fun and cherish the experience.

> *"To make flying fun,*
> *have the attitude of gratitude at altitude"*

Here are a few sample ideas of how to make normal everyday activities fun:

- Cook without socks on so when you drop something in the kitchen you have to pick it up with your toes. You can rinse off the food or utensils afterwards. This works your coordination between your brain and muscles and also helps with your balance. I know this sounds a bit weird, but who cares what someone else thinks about what you do in the kitchen. What a unique way to look at meal prep!

- While waiting for an elevator or a stoplight, estimate how long it will take for the door to close or the light to change. It's a simple game that adds a touch of excitement to routine moments.

- Try to put your socks and shoes on with your

feet in the air and not resting on anything. When you're out and your shoes become untied, you can try to tie them *without leaning against anything!* This is not as easy as it sounds. These will also help you with your balance, which is important as you get older.

- Create little songs or ditties that you sing when going through a stressful situation or even when walking, cooking or doing any activity. Singing brings joy to your heart.

- Consider getting a dog and teaching it new tricks. Or get a dog and don't teach him any tricks. Either way, get a dog. You will have more joy in your life whichever you choose.

- When making eggs, make them into monster faces for your kids by adding veggies: carrots, celery, cucumber, or fruit slices. Not only do they really like it, you will get pleasure from their joy while knowing that they are eating something nutritious. I use shredded lettuce for the hair, peppers for the mouth, grapes for the eyes, and a carrot for the nose. You can be creative and will find making eggs fun!

- Reward yourself with a treat like a bowl of ice cream or a glass of wine when tackling challenging reading material. It makes the task feel more like an accomplishment.

- When going up a flight of stairs, race to the top with whoever is with you. It adds a touch of excitement to an otherwise mundane activity. For a unique challenge, try descending stairs using as few steps as possible for each floor. Using handrails can make it safer and allows you to skip more steps.

- When you hear music, don't resist the urge to dance! Let the rhythm lift you up and move to the beat.

While setting goals is important, to get the most enjoyment, redirect your focus on the future pleasure that you will get from achieving those goals. If your goals are difficult, or may be painful for you to attempt, just think of the pain/pleasure ratio and you will be more willing to handle the pain. That ratio states that the more pleasure you achieve from something, the more pain is required to achieve it. With this theory in mind, you will enhance your resilience when you eventually overcome roadblocks to your reach your goal. You just have to keep focused on the pleasure, and then you will be able to handle any pain.

If you ask many parents what their greatest pleasure is, hopefully they will say, their children. Then if you ask them what their greatest pain is, more often than not it will also be their children. That sounds like a paradox! How can both be true? It is proof of the validity of the pain/pleasure paradox ratio.

Focusing on the pleasure in every aspect of life, while understanding that it also takes pain, will make your life more fun and increase your self-esteem.

10.
Synchronize With Others

Syncing with others is a powerful way to uplift your well-being and improve your self-esteem. We feel good because we are collaborating with others, which means we are helping other people succeed. You feel like you are part of a coordinated group, and that when your contributions make a difference, not only will the entire group will thrive, but you will to.

This is why young people gravitate towards gangs. There is a universal human desire to belong to something. However, if these groups could redirect their purpose towards constructive endeavors instead of criminal activities, the world could be a much different place.

When I was in school from 7th-12th grade, I always sang in a chorus. It always felt good to be part of something larger than yourself. Scientifically, the benefits have been proven to be as good as exercise. It calms the heart and boosts endorphin levels. Group singing boosts the production of immunoglobulin, which makes your body fight infections.

In hindsight, it's clear that individuals who sang in the chorus were very happy people. The prevalence of drug use was considerably lower than in other departments in my school. Join anything where you are part of something larger than yourself, such as: community theatre, band, orchestra, flash mob, swim team, or anything where each person plays an important role. This syncing will be a welcome boost to your self-esteem.

You could say that joining a yoga or spinning class could have the same benefits, but any of these classes would continue without having to replace you. If you left your chorus, most likely you would have to be replaced. The distinctive aspect of these groups is that they depend on every member. That integral part of being an important piece of the puzzle is what makes syncing with others one way to raise your self-esteem.

The most successful sports teams are generally the ones where they practice together and spend the off the field time becoming a cohesive unit. We can see this in basketball where one great player can make a huge difference on the outcome of the season. When that player is playing for his own statistics without caring about the success as a whole team, that team usually never makes it far into the playoffs, even though they may have the best player in the game. When they are able to play as one unit, their game is elevated. These are the teams that usually win the championship. Of course, having the best player in the game *and* having a cohesive unit will most likely provide the best outcome.

This dynamic of syncing with others is a powerful way to boost self-esteem.

11.
Exercise

Why is exercise so important for building self-esteem? It used to be that not many years ago when we wanted to eat, we had to shlep water from the river, chop down a tree for firewood, and then go out and hunt our favorite animal for dinner. Now if we are just the slightest hungry, we just dial 1-800-DoorDash and whatever you desire is delivered to our front door with no exertion whatsoever: from Chinese to vegan to hamburgers, and everything in between.

We used to have to exercise, *just to survive!* Now all we do is sit on our couch, watch Netflix, and our dinner gets delivered to us in styrofoam packaging that will outlive us by 1000 years. I understand that many people do exercise, mainly when we go to a gym to strengthen body parts that we have no need for. Then we grumble and complain when we drive to the mall and have to park a hundred feet away from the entrance.

In most societies, exercise is just not part of our daily routine, unless you reside in a city like New York, Florence or Jerusalem where walking is a common means of getting around. This contrast in lifestyles underscores the importance of exercise in our daily routine, not just for our physical health, but mainly for our mental health and well-being.

When our body is not exercising, our brains are lacking the ability to release endorphins and then it becomes very easy for us to feel sad, depressed, or to develop low self-esteem. Exercise can help you to feel good about yourself, naturally, without the need to take any drugs. Exercise is probably the most important ingredient you need to raise self-esteem. Not only do you feel physically better about yourself, but you also feel emotionally better.

Our bodies indeed produce what we can describe as "natural drugs" when we exercise, generally known as dopamine, melatonin, and serotonin. I also call these "free drugs" because they have no monetary cost and they do not have any of the negative side effects of taking drugs that are produced outside the body.

These chemicals play a significant role in our well-being. Some of the sensations, like the "runner's high," are associated with the release of these chemicals during physical activity. This high can last for several days, during which your body and mind are in a state of harmony. While your body may experience physical discomfort and soreness, you generally feel fantastic overall.

The feelings of elation, often attributed to endorphins, are, in fact, the result of various neurotransmitters and hormones working together to create a sense of well-being. So, while it may not be solely endorphins responsible for these positive feelings, they play a major role in how we feel.

Dr. David Linden, Ph.D., breaks down the phenomenon of runner's high and other effects running has on the brain.[9] Whichever case ends up being accepted in the scientific community, it doesn't really matter, because the output is all the same. If you want to have strong self-esteem and feel good about yourself, make aerobic exercise a part of your life.

When you start out on your run, your body goes through a transition: your breathing becomes heavy, and your pulse quickens as the heart pumps harder to move oxygenated blood to your muscles and brain.

As you hit your stride, your body then releases these endorphins. Although endorphins help prevent muscles from feeling pain, which is quite amazing in itself, according to Dr. Linden, it is unlikely that endorphins in the blood contribute to a euphoric feeling, or any mood change at all. Research is now showing that endorphins do not pass the blood-brain barrier.

That relaxed post-run feeling may instead be due to endocannabinoids — biochemical substances similar to cannabis, but naturally produced by the body. It seems that the more we learn about cannabis, the more beneficial it can be for us.

"Exercise has a dramatic antidepressant effect," says Linden. "It blunts the brain's response to physical and emotional stress." Besides elevating one's mood, other mental benefits include improved memory and focus.

By making running or jogging, or any aerobic exercise a regular part of your routine, you stand to earn more than just physical gains over time. "Voluntary exercise is the single best thing one can do to slow the cognitive decline that accompanies normal aging," says Linden.

---

[9] A professor of neuroscience at the Johns Hopkins University School of Medicine

As I mentioned earlier in this book, I started training for a marathon for the purpose of improving my writing and speaking ability. I believe that it plays a major factor in my creativity and energy level.

Also the type of fuel you put in your body will determine what kind of output you will get. We have a saying in our house, "junk in, junk out." If you want to start feeling good about yourself, start putting good things into your body and start your day with a run!

Following a satisfying run, it's uncommon to hear someone say that they feel miserable. The post-run experience is almost positive. Regardless of the challenges during the run, whether it's dealing with fatigue or heat, the sense of accomplishment afterward is overwhelming. The sheer joy will eclipse any physical pain. This is just like professional football players who can endure playing in blizzard conditions wearing only thin jerseys. Their passion for the game surpasses the bodies' natural aversion to freezing cold conditions, showcasing the incredible power of motivation.

Although running is the most efficient way to increase your self-esteem, walking can also be effective. Walking just takes longer to get the same effects as running, and you need to incorporate steep hills at a fast pace to get your heart rate up enough to produce these mood enhancing chemicals. Whether you choose to run or walk, make it a consistent part of your routine—be it outdoors or on a treadmill—it can yield tremendous results within a few weeks. The primary advantage is the significant improvement of self-esteem and overall health.

12. Meditation and Prayer

We are now on the last of the 12 strategies for improving low self-esteem. Although there is not one simple cure that can solve this issue, what can be of no help to one person may be the perfect remedy for another. Hopefully, no one has to focus on all 12 of these strategies to uplift themselves, but a combination of several may be necessary. Determining which approaches resonate for you, and then spending your time dedicating yourself to those specific methods is the key to having success in increasing your self-esteem.

If you are wondering why the inclusion of prayer and meditation is a remedy to low self-esteem, consider that, at times, it's essential to direct your attention towards something greater than your individual self. Meditation gives the brain a chance to process and sort through thoughts, discarding any unnecessary noise. It is like talking to yourself through your conscience. Prayer on the other hand, is connecting to a source higher than you. Instead of talking to yourself, you are talking to a divine power.

The benefits of meditation can include reduced stress, improved focus, and better emotions, which will lead to a greater sense of overall well-being. Regular meditation practice can also lead to changes in the brain's structure and function, including increased gray matter. This neurobiological effect is associated with improved self-esteem, further highlighting the advantages of incorporating meditation into one's routine.

Some individuals who claim to meditate may unknowingly be engaging in a form of prayer. They might describe it as connecting with nature, listening to their inner voice, or adopting any term that brings them comfort without identifying the entity to which they're communicating. The difference between meditation and prayer often becomes obscured between the diverse realms of religion, spirituality, and a tranquil, Zen-like state of mind.

Prayer operates on a similar principle as syncing with others; it facilitates a connection to something beyond oneself. Just as a chorus relies on your voice, or a band depends on your drumming to maintain beat and rhythm, you are playing a crucial role in something larger. This relationship thrives only when both parties actively participate. Being not just wanted, but genuinely needed in order for the relationship to flourish is one of the reasons why prayer proves beneficial for addressing low self-esteem. It's hard to have negative feelings about oneself when you recognize your contribution is not just significant, but vital. This could be one explanation why parents may often grapple less with low self-esteem issues; they have an awareness of being needed by their children.

Whether termed prayer or meditation, both involve the recognition that the world extends beyond yourself. It's an acknowledgment that one isn't in absolute control of the world, so one may as well have a more relaxed perspective.

This will help one live with less worry and anxiety. Excessive worry rarely helps a situation. Knowing this reinforces the notion that one is only in control of what they can control.

Therefore, it is imperative to know that there are only 2 things you should never worry about. They are:

1. The things you can't control. If you have no ability to control it, there is nothing you can do anyway, so why worry about it!

2. The things you can control. If you can control it, that means you can do something about it. Therefore, don't worry about it and stop using your excess energy on unnecessary anxiety.

And everything else that does not fit into these two categories? You should really worry about it!

Which means that you should never worry because almost every situation can fall into one of those two categories.

When you are flying on a plane, it is unlikely that you interview the pilot to make sure they are qualified to fly you across the continent. Instead, you trust that the pilot has 100% certainty that he knows what he is doing. This trust allows you to relax on the flight even during turbulence, at least for most people that are not afraid of flying. Similarly, entrusting yourself and having a relationship with a higher being can bring a sense of tranquility in life. Placing your trust in a higher power provides a reassuring perspective, knowing that they are in control.

I realize that if you are not a spiritual person it is hard to believe in a God. This is generally the case more with men than women. Men tend to think they run the world and everything that happens is because of their actions.

Men who are more spiritual understand they are just the steward of the gifts that God provided them.

Women often exhibit a deeper connection to spirituality, making prayer a more natural practice for them. It's a reasonable assumption that a higher proportion of women actively participate in religious gatherings compared to men.

I understand the reluctance to believe in a higher source, especially with the absence of concrete scientific evidence. However, we must also be aware that there are many beliefs we hold to be true without 100% evidence.

I recall the time when the OJ Simpson murder trial dominated television for an extended period in 1995. Despite the belief by many that he was guilty, the fundamental principle in American law is there is a presumption of innocence until proven guilty beyond a reasonable doubt

If there is a reasonable doubt, they are considered innocent. However, there does not have to be 100% uncontroversial proof of the crime. Circumstantial evidence is enough to put someone in jail. That means someone can be found guilty based only on indirect and inconclusive evidence. No one has to see the murder.

In the OJ Simpson case, there was the famous glove that did not fit, which was a bit ridiculous because it does not matter how well a glove has to fit to be used in a murder. Additionally, when a glove is soaked in blood, or any liquid, it shrinks about 15%. The biggest evidence that he murdered the victims, besides there being *no other* suspect, was his constant jealousy and stalking. Even him running away in the Ford Bronco was not enough for anyone to know that he was guilty of murder. Maybe he was driving away from the police because he had illegal drugs on him and it had nothing to do with the murder. In the end, including the gaff with the famous glove, everyone knew that he was guilty, Yet, no one saw him do it!

Is it possible for us to believe in something without seeing it? Believing in something without direct evidence is within our capacity; the key lies in managing our cognitive dissonance. It's crucial to ensure that our beliefs aren't influenced by an outcome we may find challenging. For instance, the reluctance to accept the existence of God might stem from concerns about having to become obedient to that same God.

Even if you are not sure about there being a God, or want to hedge your bets just in case, which I would guess is the majority of people, praying will transform your beliefs. Once you start to see the results, it will start to be the catalyst to an even deeper connection, prompting a desire to incorporate prayer in your life more frequently.

Praying is just like nurturing a relationship. The better relationship we have with anyone, the happier we are as people. Fostering a meaningful connection through prayer can enhance our spiritual fulfillment, but the biggest benefit will be an increase in your positive self-esteem.

In life, we are generally as happy as our worst relationship. Working on your relationship with God will help you with *all* your relationships, especially with yourself. When you show love and gratitude to the one who created you, it will be easier to show love and gratitude to yourself, and everyone else you know. If you can show gratitude to God, then it will be easier to work on your relationship with the people that *are* in your life, including yourself. Who does not want to live a life like that?

Prayer is a practice that enriches our lives, creating gratitude and connection. So when we pray to God, we are not doing it for him. Simply put, God does not need our prayers. He has everything! Prayer is just for us.

> *Imagine that a 4 year old walks into her house with a bunch of dandelions and says to her mother, "Hi mommy, happy birthday, I picked these flowers for you." Would a mother tell her daughter that they are just a bunch of weeds and to throw them in the trash? That is highly unlikely. What she may say is "Sweetheart, thank you so much! These flowers are absolutely beautiful. Let's find a special vase for them and we can put them in the middle of the table. I'm so proud of you for being so thoughtful."*

As her mother, do you need her flowers? Do you even want her flowers? Most likely not; they are a bunch of weeds! But you would never say anything negative to your daughter about the flowers. Why? Because you love your daughter and you want her to feel good about herself. Your answer expresses appreciation for the thought rather than the flowers themselves. So much so that you will stick them in a vase of water and tell your whole family how proud you are of her. By accepting the flowers, you both love each other even more.

Prayer is like you bringing God a bunch of flowers. He has no use for them just as the mother has no use for them, however, everyone is happier in the relationship because prayer is about making a connection.

Additionally, showing gratitude will help you to get what you are asking for. If you give that same daughter a cookie and she responds with a thank you, but then says to you "can I please have another cookie", what do you want to do? If you are like most people, you want to say yes! As a parent, you love it when your children say thank you, especially if they do it like they really mean it. It creates a desire for you to want to fulfill their requests and give them everything they want, as long as it's good for them.

Maybe you won't give them 3 or 4 cookies, especially if it is close to dinner, but you will make every attempt to make them happy.

These ideas parallel our relationship with God. God won't give us everything we want, even though we desire it or think we need it.

If you ever observe confident young adults embark on their journey into the world, they most likely had healthy relationships with their parents. Conversely, young adults grappling with anxiety and fear often trace their struggles back to strained relationships with their parents. Their parents might have been physically present, but emotionally distant, or the dysfunction within their family dynamic could have hindered the development of a healthy and meaningful connection.

If we want to go out into the world as confident, happy people, it's best if we have cultivated a healthy relationship with our parents. Part of that relationship is gratitude between both parents and children. This is why it is so important to forgive your parents if they were the cause of your low self-esteem. If that relationship is dysfunctional, your life may be dysfunctional.

Then there is also a relationship with the One who created us, which many people call our Father in heaven. He is called that because without him, we would not exist! Even though we have parents who procreated and gave birth to us, God is part of that miracle that made us.

This relationship is not a one-way street. Just like the relationship with parents is not a one-way street. The same as there is a proper way for a child to ask for a second cookie, there is a way to ask properly for something from the Creator. The key lies in knowing how to approach and articulate your requests clearly.

Consider a scenario where God made himself known to you. For example, let's say He appeared to you in a mirage, spoke to you, or made it known to you without any doubt that he exists. Would this reshape the dynamics of your life? It would probably take away your free will. Knowing that there is someone watching over you would give you a bit more confidence in life, but it would also make you turn into a robot. You would adhere to any directive without the freedom to explore personal choices.

It is kind of like driving down the New Jersey Turnpike and about 1/2 a mile in front of you see a cop with a radar gun pointed in your direction. What is the first thing you do *without any hesitation whatsoever?* If you are like me, you hit the brake and *then* look at your speedometer. This is what is called not having free will. You make decisions without any thought process because of the anticipated consequences. That is like being in metaphorical jail. I highly doubt that is the relationship that anyone wants.

Can you imagine dating or marrying someone that was completely subservient to you? Picture a scenario where every request or suggestion is met with a simple "yes, dear." Unless you are a control freak or have narcissist traits, you would not want to live life with someone like that. The ideal partner is someone capable of independent thought, who can make decisions autonomously. Seeking a companion with the ability to think for themselves and express differing opinions adds depth and richness to a relationship.

Free will is an important part of being a human. It is why we get pleasure when we accomplish things that we chose ourselves. Imagine building a software company from the ground up, transforming it into a multi-billion-dollar conglomerate – the sense of accomplishment and pleasure derived from this will would be immense.

Contrast this with a scenario where a father hands over to his son the same company on his 21st birthday. While there may be some initial excitement, the pleasure derived from this accomplishment would pale in comparison. True satisfaction comes from the choices and actions we make independently. The pleasure that the son receives pales in comparison to the pleasure that the father received. This is the same with our belief in God. You have to find it on your own, without coercion. That is why he does not come to us in our dreams, or anytime, to let us know that he exists. You would then lose your free will *and* your pleasure.

How do we know that pleasure is an important part of our life? I am going to give you two compelling reasons. What is the number one factor that determines the decisions that you make in life? That decision is based on one thing. Will it bring me pleasure? Do I eat the chocolate cake or do I eat the raw broccoli? Which one will bring me the most pleasure? For most of us, the cake is going to win out because it's a source of greater pleasure, unless the broccoli is stir fired in teriyaki and garlic sauce. Our choices, whether big or small, are intrinsically tied to the pursuit of pleasure. People that understand how to live with pleasure are not struggling with low self-esteem.

Even if you choose to go to the dentist for a cavity or root canal, you are only going for the pleasure of preventing yourself from pain in the future.

Secondly, understanding the first place in the world where man was created will give us a clue. The first dwelling place for man in Hebrew is called "Gan Eden", or what most people translate it to as "The Garden of Eden." The word "Eden" (ee-den) is just the transliteration of the Hebrew word Eden (eh-den). More accurately, the translation of "Gan Eden" is "The Garden of Pleasure." It's not a far fetch to derive that the real purpose for our existence is based on us having pleasure, or He would have placed us in a place called "The Garden of Hell."

God gave Adam and Eve the free will to choose to eat from any tree, but warned them not to eat from the tree of knowledge. It's that free will that gives us pleasure in life. No free will, no pleasure.

You are free to choose to either believe in Him or not to believe. That is a personal choice. But if you believe that there is even a small chance that there is a Creator, you may want to start to form a relationship with Him. This will open the door to a deeper connection where higher levels of pleasure and strong self-esteem are achievable. Low self-esteem is not part of creation. It is just derived from our own thoughts. This is why if you can change your mindset, you can change your life.

So how does one pray to the Creator of the universe, recognizing that he does not need our prayers? This is the answer to the $10 Million-Dollar question that will be a major step in repairing your low self-esteem.

Prayer, in this context, is not about only fulfilling your needs, but about connection. This is why believing and praying to God is not a religion, it's a relationship.

"This is why believing and praying to God is not a religion, it's a relationship"

God loves those that love others, including themselves.

When I used to hire babysitters for my children, each teenager would engage with them differently. Some would sit on the couch and play on their phone by themselves, and others would play games with my kids, bake cookies, and show them how to clean up after dinner.

I recall once hiring a 14-year-old babysitter for our children. It was just a few weeks after the birth of our fifth child in seven years. We were planning on taking the baby out with us, not expecting a young girl to want to watch an infant along with 4 other small children. When she came over, she insisted she wanted to watch all of the children, including the baby. She was extremely mature for her age and she not only cared for them, but also engaged in activities, like making muffins and playing games. She was amazing! We loved her! Of course it is easy to see why we loved her so much. We loved her because she loved our children. This is the same with God, He loves those that love his children.

We have to get along with everyone in this world. We are not on an island where we can do what we want without any consequences. If we love other people, God will then love us back just like we love our favorite babysitter. Wouldn't you rather be the favorite babysitter in God's eyes?

This also means that we should love ourselves, just like we love other people. A child that comes from an abusive home will always love their parents, it is themselves that they do not love. This is why when we do not love ourselves, it is almost as if we are abusing ourselves.

But first we must answer the common question, why bad things happen to good people. This can be a barrier from people opening their hearts to the notion that there is a God. After that, we will delve into the four steps of prayer. All this prep work is needed so when we do discuss prayer, you will have much more clarity on who it is you are praying to and what you are praying for.

Why do bad things happen to good people?

I will occasionally encounter questions like "Why did the Holocaust happen?" or questions about very difficult personal hardships, all of which ultimately lead to a common underlying question—why would God permit such adversity? How could God let this happen to me?

If you do not believe in God, you would never ask a question about God because how can you ask a question about something you don't believe in. I would never ask a question about BigFoot or the Loch Ness Monster. I know they don't exist so why would I ever ask about them. When someone questions if there is a God, even though they say they don't believe in Him, there must be something in the back of their mind that is causing this latent curiosity. What it usually boils down to is their lack of clarity on how to articulate their anger from a challenge they faced. It is very easy in this instance to confuse not believing in God with actually being mad at God.

A young man, dressed in the casual attire typical of American teenagers, strolls along the busy streets of Mea Shearim, a deeply religious neighborhood in Jerusalem. Although coming from a non-religious background, he finds himself delving deeper into his Jewish heritage. Suddenly, a man dressed in traditional religious attire points at him and yells, "You're not a Jew!"

Shocked by the encounter, the young man, visibly upset, runs to his Rabbi overseeing his journey.

The Rabbi gently asks the young man, "Why are you upset? If you were to say the same thing to him, what do you think he would do? He would laugh, dismissing it without a second thought."

When one lives with clarity in who they are as a person, they won't let someone else's negative comment bother them.

In Israel, there's a notable Kibbutz known for professing its anti-religious stance. They claim that they don't believe in God, which they have a right to do. (On a side note, if you have ever been to Israel, and learned about its survival, you would have a hard time *not* believing in God). Ironically, what is funny about their lack of belief in God, is that they hold a BBQ every year on Yom Kippur. This is the holiest day of the year for Jews, in which Jews do not eat or drink for 25 hours.

If they truly did not believe in God, they would never coincide their BBQ with Yom Kippur. The deliberate choice of that day suggests a motive rooted in spite, signaling the message that "we reject God." They are trying to send a message that we don't believe in God so look what we are doing, we are desecrating a Jews holiest day.

Imagine if you lived in a country where they celebrated a holiday where everyone gets together to watch a 4 hour football game, drinks beer, and eats wings, guacamole, and chips and salsa. If you did not like the sport, would you do something to show your distaste for the game? Maybe you would encourage large groups of like minded people to protest outside the stadium to convince other people how dangerous or stupid the game is? I highly doubt it. You probably just have a normal Sunday where you would go shopping instead of watching the Super Bowl. For you, it is not an emotional issue because you don't care. With the case of the anti-religious Kibbutz, if it was not an emotionally charged issue for them, they would just ignore the holiday and it would just be a regular work day.

The question someone is really asking when questioning the existence of God is, "Why did this struggle happen to me?" For those who have endured tragedy or significant challenges, this could be the most crucial answer they are looking for.

The very first thing you need to ask yourself when wrestling with the question of why did this tragedy happen to me; is your question an emotional one, or an intellectual one? If it is an intellectual one, such as why did I break my leg, then there is an answer for you. If it is a highly emotional question, like the death of someone you love very much, then there is no answer that I, or anyone can give you that is going to help. Emotions take a long time to heal and until significant time has elapsed, there really is no answer that is going to help you.

Consider this scenario; a loving spouse has passed away and they are at the funeral crying, leaning over the casket and sobbing "Why, why, why." An acquaintance of the spouse comes over and kneels next to them and says to them in a quiet, somber voice, "I am so sorry for your loss, but your spouse died because their 3rd ventricle of their heart stopped working and the blood clot that formed traveled to the brain and eventually caused a massive stroke in which the brain stopped signaling the heart to beat causing a failure in the intake of oxygen which caused them to die." They respond, "Oh, thank you, I feel so much better now!"

That would seem ridiculous. It seems ridiculous because there is no answer for the grieving spouse! No person will find solace in the detailed medical explanation of why they died. When you are highly emotional, there is no answer that will ever satisfy you. When someone asks the question about why the Holocaust happened, there is no answer that anyone can give that will satisfy them. It is because they are asking from emotions, not intellect. On the other hand, if you are asking from an intellectual point of view, then there may be some answers. Intellectually, you are asking why bad things happen to good people. That may be hard to hear when it refers to the depth of the inhumanity of the Holocaust, the October 7th massacre in Israel, or many of the mass murders happening in schools in America.

Intellectually, there are 3 answers to why bad things happen to good people.

The first answer is negligence. Negligence is why bad things happen to good people. In many cases, this explains the occurrence of unfortunate events, though it's crucial to note that this explanation doesn't fully address the depth of the Holocaust and similar disasters.

A business associate recently told me a distressing story about his wife. Her ankle was broken and she is potentially crippled for the rest of her life. She was riding in a golf cart with her drunk cousin and he was driving recklessly which caused the golf cart to flip over resulting in severe injuries.

After a month in a hospital and lots of physical therapy, she is still struggling with the injuries. This all happened because of negligence on her cousin's part. Does she have any blame? If she was aware that he was drinking, then maybe there is some blame on her part for allowing herself to get into a golf cart with him. Negligence becomes apparent in situations where individuals knowingly expose themselves to potential harm. As discussed earlier in the book, self destructive behaviors are quite common for people with low self-esteem.

This is always relevant when car accidents happen. Usually there is someone at fault, but even in many of those cases, the driver that is absolved from wrongdoing could have taken measures to prevent the accident; either by driving slower or anticipating the action of other drivers more carefully. Not everyone has this nuanced ability and awareness to predict future actions on the road, but that is what a good driver does, predicts potential accidents in advance and takes precautions to avoid them.

The second reason why bad things happen to good people is measure for measure. This is what people refer to as karma. This concept suggests that there is a reciprocal relationship between our actions and their consequences. If you treat others badly, then you will be treated badly by others. Our actions are done with a mirror right in front of us. Whatever we do has a corresponding impact right back onto our lives.

I was teaching a group of young women recently and as soon as I started, a young lady raised her hand and said, "I don't believe in God, I believe everything happens for a reason." Try dissecting that comment for a minute. How can everything happen for a reason, but there is no entity who determines what that reason is? What she could have said is "I don't believe in God, everything in the world is random."

This is akin to what we discussed in an earlier chapter on how you can cause others to have low self-esteem. Maybe your actions toward someone else are affecting the "karma" that is coming right back at you. In this case, something must be in control of that karma because believing in karma and *not* believing in God is a contradiction.

The third reason why bad things happen to good people is that it's good for you. This may be hard to accept, but this is true if seen in a broader perspective. This viewpoint is exemplified by historical events, such as the Holocaust, where the horrors faced by the Jewish nation played a role in the restoration of the land of Israel. In essence, it suggests that sometimes, from a larger vantage point, challenging experiences contribute to positive developments.

I always hear stories of people who were turned down for a job, or by a school, or even by the person they are dating. As soon as one door is closed, suddenly other opportunities open up that they may have never noticed if they were busy with their first opportunity. There is a saying that for every door God closes, another one opens up.

So far in this chapter, we have delved into several key concepts that should pave the way for our exploration of prayer:

- Recognition that the world extends beyond your existence and you have no control of it
- Worrying causes unneeded stress
- We can believe in God without actually having irrefutable evidence
- Circumstantial evidence satisfies our convictions for many of our beliefs
- Women and men are not made up of the same spiritual muscles
- Prayer is about nurturing a relationship

- Gratitude to God mirrors the parent-child relationship
- God gave us free will so we can get pleasure
- Humans were created for pleasure
- When we take pleasure in everything God gave us, we will have positive self-esteem
- God loves those that love his children, so we should definitely learn to love others, especially ourselves
- There are 3 reasons why bad things happen to good people. If it is an emotional question, there is no answer. If it is an intellectual question, then there are 3 answers: negligence, karma, & it's good for you

Hopefully, this may be a major shift in your perspective suggesting that adversity may, in some way, be beneficial, including having low self-esteem. With this in mind, we can make a paradigm shift and live with the gratitude that everything that happens to us is good for us.

The 4 steps to prayer to cure your low self-esteem

As we approach the final remedy for addressing low self-esteem, I hope that the preceding 11 strategies have been valuable in guiding you towards gaining traction to more positive self-esteem, and ultimately a more fulfilling life.

If prayer is a path you are considering to help you improve your low self-esteem, it would be helpful to know the steps involved so you could significantly enhance the likelihood of getting your prayers answered.

We will use the acronym REPEAT to make it easier for you to remember the steps involved in prayer. Acronyms are particularly useful for retaining information, especially after attending a class or lecture where the content may be overwhelming. How many times have you attended a fabulous lecture and wanted to give the content over, but you could not remember it?

This word is also relevant since prayer is a practice you can repeat as many times as you want and also do it anywhere in the world.

When you decide to engage in prayer, you first need to remove the two E's, which represent Envy and Ego. This is the only sincere way to connect during your moments of prayer.

Envy, in essence, implies a belief that there is an error in the divine world and that God made a mistake. Envy means that someone else has something that you desire, or that you don't want them to have. Either way, the world is not working the way you think it should be and this misalignment in the grand scheme of the universe is causing you to be unhappy. It is hard to have clarity praying to God when you think he made a mistake.

Envy and jealousy are often used interchangeably, though there are nuanced distinctions between the two. Envy typically denotes a desire for another person's possessions, qualities, or position in life. Many individuals use "jealous" in a similar context, such as when saying "I am envious of his good fortune" or "I am jealous of his good fortune," with little change in meaning.

However, where envy falls short, jealousy comes into play, particularly in situations involving suspicions of romantic infidelity. When someone suspects that their partner may be involved with another individual, they are described as experiencing jealousy. In such instances, "He is a jealous husband" cannot be substituted with "He is an envious husband" without a significant shift in meaning.

Regardless of whether one opts for envy or jealousy, both terms imply dissatisfaction with the status quo. These emotions frequently originate from feelings of insecurity.

Ego is essential for our survival and for thriving as a species. It provides the drive to earn a living and raise a family. However, when the ego becomes excessive, the quest for recognition and honor can lead to an inflated perspective of oneself. One cannot be real with prayer when they think the world revolves around them. This mindset, which probably stems from low self-esteem, often results in trouble, as evidenced by many examples of individuals who have abused their power. A principle to bear in mind and one that I live with constantly is "your ego is not your amigo." This simple mantra serves as a reminder to keep our egos in check, preventing them from becoming enlarged. Limiting our ego increases a dose of humility. Plus people won't think of you as a jerk.

"Your Ego Is Not Your Amigo"

Enlarged egos often serve as the root cause of broken relationships and business failures. It's a realization that often becomes clearer with age – the recognition that one's enlarged ego might have been a source of numerous setbacks in life that could have been avoided. Unfortunately, I have been witness to this too many times in my life. I have seen the eventual outcomes of people whose egos were enlarged. Eventually, the outcome is never positive for their lives.

True contentment arises from being grateful for what one has. When the ego demands a constant pursuit of material possessions, such as expensive cars or clothing, it typically stems from a lack of self-esteem. Individuals with robust self-esteem, who love themselves no matter what they drive or wear, are less prone to allowing their ego to dictate their lives. Their sense of self-worth doesn't hinge on constant validation through their possessions or achievements

I like to think that God gave us each a check at birth, representing our array of gifts and talents. Our job in life is to "cash" that check. This idea of a "divine check" encapsulates our physical and creative potential. When we are using our talents to their fullest, it's not us asserting how great we are, but rather a process of cashing in on the skills that God gave us.

Tiger Woods started hitting golf balls from the remarkable young age of 2 years old. If I had started hitting golf balls at 2 years old, would I be as good as Tiger Woods? Not only would I not be as good, making it on the PGA Tour would have been a bigger miracle than the splitting of the Red Sea! Hitting a golf ball into a small hole in as few shots as possible was not a skill that God endowed me with. That was not included in the "check" that God wrote to me. He did give me some other unique skills that have set me on my own course: my gift of helping people and navigating relationships more effectively. This skill set has proven invaluable to create an awesome marriage for myself. While I might not wield a golf club like Tiger Woods, the gifts God gave me upon have paved the way for a fulfilling and meaningful journey.

Imagine going to a bank with a five-thousand dollar check and telling the teller to just give you four-thousand dollars. That would seem insane! That is exactly what you are doing when you don't reach your potential in life. I can guarantee you that having low-self esteem was not part of the deposit that God made into your, metaphorically speaking, personal checking account.

This perspective acknowledges that one's skills and abilities would not exist without the gifts from God. By understanding that the size of the check is not a measure of superiority, you will live with more gratitude and humility, which will lead you to more happiness.

Now that we have removed envy and ego from the equation, the last 4 letters of our acronym *REPEAT* are **R-P-A-T.** They stand for: Recognize, Praise, Ask and Thanks. Let's explore this framework so we can gain the clarity to develop positive self-esteem.

During one of the Jewish holidays, a prayer service in a synagogue was delayed due to the requirement of having 10 men to form what is referred to as a minyan. They were only 9 men, so they were just 1 short. One of the men went outside to the street to see if he could discover some random Jewish man walking by to help. Soon enough, a man walked by and the congregant asked if he was Jewish. The man said that he was and the congregant asked him if he could help make their minyan. The man answered "I'm sorry, but I don't believe in organized religion." The congregant answered, "If it was so organized, do you think I would be out here?"

Recognize - Prayer is a deeply personal act that is driven by three objectives. One is to ask for something you want, the second is for help or guidance on an issue. The third is expressing gratitude for whatever it is you are thankful for. Whichever you are doing, the first step to prayer is just recognizing that there is a God who you are praying to. You aren't praying to a Buddha statue because a figurine made of clay cannot do anything for you. You are not praying to a prayer book or a person dressed in a long robe standing on a giant stage! It is God whom we are praying to. This is the clarity you need to make your prayers real.

Some people will spend anywhere from just a few minutes to an hour just thinking about all the miracles that exist in this world because of God. Some of these are: our unique strands of DNA, black holes, the perfect alignment of our earth in our solar system, to all the unfathomable connections and synapses in our brain that allow us to function. Unfortunately, sometimes we only become aware of this when we have a health issue or are in danger.

There is an adage that there are no atheists in a foxhole. It is only when someone is in times of distress that they will be inclined to reach out to God. Since most of us live without imminent danger, the need to call out to God may not seem so urgent. All of the miracles we see everyday become "normal" and then we lose sight of it being a miracle. We chalk it up to being "nature" and therefore God is not involved. Therefore, we don't feel the need to recognize that there is a God.

As explored earlier, how close we are to someone will influence the likelihood of receiving help from them when needed. We don't want to be in a predicament where you have to call out for help and no one answers because the person doesn't have a close relationship with you.

Who would willingly dash through the flames of a burning building to rescue a stranger? The odds of such a heroic act increase significantly when the person in peril is your closest friend. Elevate the stakes further, and there is no doubt in your mind that you would risk your life when it involves a family member. The ratio of your willingness to face life-threatening situations appears to correlate directly with the depth of the relationship; the stronger the connection, the greater the inclination to assist, and, if necessary, to sacrifice one's own life.

Therefore, establishing a relationship with God will put you in the position of influence when it comes time for you to make a request from him. This way he will be more inclined to respond easily to your pleas.

Acknowledging who you are praying to is the foremost step if you want to have clarity on prayer. You should tell yourself that you are not praying to a political figure or a celebrity. Instead, your connection is to the architect of existence. This will bring focus and depth to your prayers.

Many popular movies don't specially mention God even though spirituality is the central theme. Both Princess Lea and Darth Vader are always referring to the force. Although Harrison Ford's character, Hans Solo is skeptical of it, "May the force be with you" is the recurring theme throughout the entire series.

In the Avatar movie, the planet Pandora is ruled by the Great Mother, Eywa, the goddess who permeates everything on the planet. Harry Potter is basically a movie about those who believe and those who don't. Muggles are those who don't believe in wizards while the wizards have to go to Hogwarts to learn "incantations", or what is referred in Yeshiva's and Seminaries as Brachas (blessings). Just as Harry Potter says "Abracadabra", its roots most likely come from the ancient Jewish Language, Aramaic. Avada Kedavra means "I will create as I speak."

Whether or not the Force, Eywa, or Harry Potter have to do with God, all one has to do is look right beneath the surface of these movies and see underlying spirituality.

A man is driving to an important appointment in bustling New York City. Looking for a parking space is weighing heavily on his mind. Having no luck finding one, he becomes desperate and calls out, "Please God, I need a parking space so I am not late!" Suddenly, he sees a front bumper of a car start to pull away from the curb in front of him. In a split second, a parking spot opens up. The man pulls right in then says to himself, "Forget it God, I don't need your help"

In this moment, the man experiences the interaction between his immediate needs and gratitude. His initial plea for God's help is met with a quick solution, yet the ensuing declaration reveals a common human tendency. Once immediate needs are fulfilled, there's a propensity to forget about God. We will certainly have improved self-esteem once we recognize that God is there to help us when needed.

Praise - Praise can be easily confused with gratitude, but there is a nuanced difference. Praise is the act of expressing approval for someone's actions or qualities. It's like saying "Good job!" Praise is used to enhance relationships and to help encourage and motivate others.

When my children clean the kitchen, I always try to make sure I offer both praise and thanks. While thanking them is important and shows my appreciation, praise will resonate more and have a better impact. I convey to them that they are doing a great job and are making my counters sparkling clean.

The confusion between praise and gratitude may arise due to some similarities in their expressions of positivity and acknowledgment. Recognizing the nuanced differences will give you more clarity.

The following story illustrates the difference between praise and gratitude.

The Super Bowl, A Sports Bookie, and Glory to God

One day, my Rabbi's wife, Lori Palatnik, was notified that she had $50 in an account of a sports bookie. It was left over from when her nephew used her email address to play poker online. Lori consulted her Rabbi about the moral implications of gambling. He reassured her, explaining that since it wasn't her money to begin with and the bookie would not return the money, she could only use it for placing a bet. The ultimatum was clear: use it or lose it.

The Super Bowl was on the horizon and the contest was between the Philadelphia Eagles vs the New England Patriots. Lori was interested in the proposition bets because they were the most interesting. You can bet on almost anything, from predicting the coin flip, to speculating who catches the most balls, or even the length of the longest field goal attempt. What caught her eye was the choice of what the winning quarterback would say to the reporter immediately after the game. Lori decided to bet on the choice of "Thanking God."

After the Eagles beat Tom Brady's Patriots, the winning quarterback, Nick Foles, was immediately interviewed by a reporter on the field. The first thing that Nick Foles said into the mic "All Glory Belongs to God." Lori heard this and was elated that she had cinched her bet! However, her enthusiasm was short-lived. The next day, she went online to check her winnings and to her surprise, her bet was labeled as pending. A few days later, the website said that she had lost. Determined to rectify what seemed like an error, Lori promptly called the bookie to challenge the decision. Despite her attempts to persuade them that she had won, they insisted on reviewing the matter. A day later, the website said, "No bet." They put the money back into the account and Lori was bummed out. After some time, she came to terms in her mind that they were correct in their decision. "All Glory Belongs to God" is *not* thanking God. That is praising God. It is important to understand the difference in order to have clarity in prayer.

Ask -This step in prayer is arguably the easiest since all you have to do is ask for what you want, but the challenge is in receiving the answer you want. Your prayer can range from anywhere from getting a date to desiring something as specific as a brand-new red Lamborghini. Regardless of the nature of your request, it's essential to approach prayer with the clarity that you are indeed asking for something. When you make your request, it's crucial to have the expectation that God is going to give you what you want. If you do not expect the answer to be yes, then you are not praying with clarity. Why should you bother praying for something if you have no expectation to get it?

God will answer your prayer; it's just that the answer might not be a "no." Sometimes a "no" is the best answer for you, even though you don't understand the reasons why.

What you want and what you need becomes pivotal when praying. God will certainly give you what you need, but not always what you want. I want a Ferrari, but I don't *need a* Ferrari. With low self-esteem in mind, understanding that God gives you what is good for you is a key element in increasing self-esteem.

What do you need to do to get your prayers answered? Just as there are 4 steps to prayer, there are also 4 questions you have to ask yourself to get your prayers answered in the way you want.

The 4 Questions you must ask yourself to get what you want

1. What is your **M**otivation?
2. Are you making an **E**ffort?
3. Are you **E**xpecting a yes?
4. Are you willing to **T**ransform yourself?

The acronym *MEET* encapsulates the four essential questions, similar to having a meeting with God. This acronym serves as a reminder that just as in any meeting, there's a specific goal or outcome you aim to achieve. In this "divine" meeting room, the objective is not merely to have God answer your prayers, but to answer with a resounding yes!

What is your motivation for asking what you want?

Understanding the motivation behind your desires is a crucial first step in the process. Begin by asking yourself: What truly motivates my request? Is it born out of a genuine need, or is it a pursuit driven by the desires of my ego?

For example, there are many people who want to get married, but are having a hard time finding someone to tie the knot with. To gain clarity on what is the motivation of your request, ask yourself *why* you want to get married?

If your answer is so someone can make you breakfast and do your laundry, then you should hire a butler, they are much cheaper. Most people who want to get married are looking for someone to fulfill their needs. When you change your motivation from wanting your needs fulfilled to wanting to fulfill *someone else's needs,* then your motivation has changed from selfish desires to selfless desires. This will likely increase your chance of getting the answer you want.

When your prayer revolves around having money so you can buy the latest fashionable clothing, it questions the source of your motivation. I always convey to my students to ask themselves whether you would still buy a Chanel purse, Prada shoes, or an Armani suit if no one else would ever see you wearing them. If the answer is a resounding no, it uncovers your motivation. Consider the underlying intention behind your desire for fashion. Is it primarily driven by the external validation and opinions of others? By honestly evaluating the core motivation, you gain insight into whether your aspirations are centered on personal satisfaction or external approval. This self-awareness can guide your prayers to be more authentic, leading to more meaningful and satisfying outcomes.

Consider applying the same question to the desire for an expensive luxury sedan or sports car: Would you still buy it if no one would ever see you drive it? This scenario aligns with the central theme highlighted earlier in this book — the greatest prison you put yourself in is worrying about what other people think of you. If the motivation behind desiring an expensive sports car is solely to attract more dates, this motivation may lack sincerity. In such cases, the likelihood of receiving the fancy car you ask for in your prayers diminishes. By striving for motivations rooted in authenticity, you increase the probability of your prayers being met with a yes.

Are you making an effort?

Are you actively putting in the effort needed to complement your prayers? The adage "God helps those who help themselves" underscores the importance of your own effort.

Imagine an acquaintance at your office gets a few people from work to help them move. As you are lugging boxes and furniture for hours, the recipient of the move is on the phone the whole time, not even lifting a box. You are probably very annoyed because you feel like you are being taken advantage of. What are you going to tell them the next time they ask you for help? Most likely you'll tell them to take a hike! The same is true for your prayers. By actively contributing for whatever it is you want, you create a partnership, increasing the odds of you getting help in the future.

Another way to help with your effort is to pray out loud in a quiet whisper, versus just thinking them. You may ask, can't God just read my mind? I have heard this question many times because it is more convenient when one doesn't have to actually verbalize what they want. The assumption here is that God possesses the ability to comprehend what you are thinking. He is God, for God's sake! Shouldn't he be able to read your mind? The answer is He *can* read your mind!

The reason why you may not want to pray out loud is you may feel kind of strange mumbling to yourself. You may feel like you are one of those people having a private conversation with their earpiece attached. At first glance you think they are a crazy homeless person who walks around on the street screaming to themselves. It is only after you walk by them that you realize they are on their phone.

You don't have to pray out loud for God to hear you, but if you don't pray out loud, that means he has to read your mind to know what you are asking for. The question you have to ask yourself; do you really want God reading your mind?

I don't know about you, but from my perspective, unless you're in the same category as Moses or Mother Theresa, there are a lot of impure thoughts that someone could possibly have. This is not indicative of a bad person, but just a reflection of being human; sometimes we can't help ourselves and have thoughts that don't really represent who we are as people!

What is not good is if someone *acted* on those thoughts. So unless you want God reading your mind and all the schmutz that goes through it, it's better for you to speak your prayers. That way you can keep your thoughts to yourself and if there is something you want God to hear, you'll speak it, even if it's very softly.

Are you expecting a yes?

Are you praying really believing that he is not only going to answer you, but actually give you what you want? Being authentic in prayer involves truly believing that your requests can be fulfilled. It's essential to recognize that God has the power to grant a wide range of requests, from significant life changes like bringing you massive wealth to smaller everyday matters such as finding your misplaced car keys or stopping a mosquito bite from itching. The key lies in having a mindset acknowledging the vastness of capabilities that God has. This is why praise is an important aspect of prayer. Knowing that nothing is too big or too small for him increases the clarity in your prayers.

Imagine a scenario where you ask your father for some money for a school field trip to a local museum. The school is asking each student to bring twenty-five cents for the modest entrance fee. The day before the trip, you ask your father for the money. In this situation, it's inconceivable to imagine your father saying no. His love and support for you to participate in school activities makes a negative response seem highly unlikely. This is how you should be thinking about prayer. God loves you just like your father and you never expect him to turn down his child for something so small.

In a contrasting scenario, your father is the president and founder of a large Wall Street investment bank. Throughout your life, he has emphasized the importance of hard work and encouraged you to apply for a job at his company after graduation. He had always inferred to you that you'll start at the entry level and work your way up. Following his advice, on the day of your graduation, you head to the human resources office to start your job. To your surprise, the woman at the desk says to you that there are currently no job openings. Initially in a bit of shock, you tell the woman that you are the boss's son. She calls his office and then confirms with you that no opportunities are currently available.

In both these scenarios you should be shocked beyond belief that your father did give you the quarter or hire you at his company. This is the feeling that you need to have when you pray and don't get what you ask for. If you are not shocked, then you're not being real with prayer. God has the capacity to give you anything and there is nothing too small or too large; from something as small as a penny, to the most profound gift, your life.

Thanks - The last part of the 4 steps to prayer is straightforward—expressing gratitude to God, regardless of the answer. Don't wait to see if your request was answered with a yes or a no before thanking Him. Thank him as soon as you ask. This demonstrates our trust that His decisions are for whatever is best for us.

There is an intriguing concept brought down in the Jewish Talmud that we should be thanking God for all the good he gives us and all the bad. This concept seems a bit hard to understand for some. Why should we thank God for all the bad things in our life? Thanking God for giving us cancer, or getting into a car accident? At its essence lies the belief that for every adversity, there are opportunities for growth and it will eventually be good for us. This is a very high level of gratitude and one that everyone should strive for.

We can get to this level by stopping to think of ourselves all the time and start thanking instead. The only difference between think and thank is one letter. Just take out the "I" and switch it for an "A". The "I" means we are selfishly only thinking of ourselves and the "A" means we are thanking the Almighty instead. When we switch from what I think I need, to what the Almighty gives us what we need, will be the catalyst to living in clarity. God will give you what you need, not what you want.

> *"God will give you want you need,*
> *not what you want"*

When your knowledge of what God gives to us is good for us deepens, our positive self-esteem will then flourish naturally. That positive self-esteem will then lay the foundation for increased resilience. Then the more resilient we become at handling life's challenges, the more it will eventually lead to our profound happiness. When we are happy, we will then have an easier time showing gratitude, which starts the process again. This interconnected circle of growth creates a powerful flywheel, gaining momentum and spinning faster with each expression of gratitude and influencing our capacity to confront and overcome life's many challenges.

The Flywheel Of Gratitude

- Expressing gratitude to God and knowing he will give us what is good for us will lead us to…
- Deepening of our positive self-esteem, which will lead us to…
- Increased resilience at handling challenges, which will lead us to…
- Our profound happiness, which will lead us to…
- An even easier time showing gratitude, which will start the process all over again.

My heartfelt wish for all my readers is that you uncover strategies within this book that will transform your life. May these insights ignite the inner fire that has always been within you, waiting to shine. Like a perfect diamond, may you become a beacon of radiant light, filled with positive energy that emanates love and warmth to everyone you meet. This will be your new reality—a world brimming with joy and happiness. You will *Never Feel Unloved Again.*

Author's Notes

During the writing of this book, a war has broken out between Hamas and Israel. The Jewish people have just had the deadliest day since the Holocaust. On Saturday morning, October 7th, 2023, thousands of Hamas terrorists came over the border and slaughtered over 1200 people. Where I live in Jerusalem has been relatively calm, except the occasional missile siren that alerts us to run to our bomb shelters. Being here now is putting tremendous amounts of strain on how I feel mentally and emotionally, and I know I am not the only one that feels this way. How does one manage the high anxiety that comes from being in a war?

Since this is happening while I am in the middle of writing this book, it has allowed me to put some of my cures to low self-esteem into action. Even though this duress may be worse than a typical case of low self-esteem, I need to find ways to help my spirits, and fortunately, these same cures will work with the worry and major anxiety that many are going through now.

For starters, the best way for me to help myself is to stay distanced from social media, which is part of the cure of

Controlling My Exposure. There are so many videos of gruesome images that if I am not careful, I could plunge into a depressive state. I also stay away from the news most of the day. Obviously, the first few days you could not keep your eyes off of what was going on, but as time went on, the influx of meaningful information diminished. Continuous engagement with every news conference or op-ed piece doesn't contribute to my well-being or improve the overall situation. Although I can't completely avoid social media, I've significantly curtailed my usage to alleviate anxiety.

I was at a recent Zoom meeting focused on local security in Jerusalem. It quickly became apparent that attending it was a mistake. The presenter emphasized worst-case scenarios, painting a bleak picture of widespread attacks by the local Arab population. While acknowledging the reality of such possibilities, especially after October 7th, the presentation only raised my anxiety level. In hindsight, I realized I should have chosen to watch something that raised my spirits instead. In prioritizing my mental well-being, controlling anxiety takes precedence. I've discovered that listening to music or watching scenes from my favorite comedies has been helpful in making me feel better. While I cannot speak to its efficacy for low self-esteem, it has proven to be a valuable coping mechanism for managing anxiety.

Being a casual runner, I decided to increase my *Exercise* during this time. A runner's high is when the body and soul are in sync together, and I really need that source of solace. Even though it is hard to gather the motivation to want to run, or do any exercise, I remain focused on the pleasure that I will receive from finishing a 3-4 mile run. This aids me in maintaining my sanity amid the chaos and also helps to produce the essential "Happy Drugs" in my brain providing a much needed boost during these tough times.

I decided to *List My Attributes* that I have in my life, particularly those that can't be bought. Compiling a list of everything I am grateful for serves as a powerful tool. For instance, I find solace in the fact that I didn't lose any loved ones in the recent tragedy and that none of my immediate family is on the front lines of the battle. Acknowledging and appreciating these aspects helps to center and ground me during these challenging times.

I am blessed to have a lot in my life and I must have gratitude for what I have. It is so easy to be hateful of your enemy at this time. So I have to keep saying to myself, be grateful instead of hateful. Being grateful for what you have will bring a sense of ease to your mind, at least a little bit, and help you through situations that create massive anxiety. Internalizing hate and keeping it in will tear apart your emotions and make it hard for you to move forward in life. Nothing is getting accomplished when you are blaming others for your problems.

Despite not considering myself particularly spiritual, I've found unexpected comfort in visiting the Western Wall and engaging with psalms that have endured for thousands of years. Incorporating psalms into while I *Pray* has brought a sense of clarity, emphasizing the belief that everything, whether perceived as good or bad, emanates from the Creator. I know it's hard to see His kindness in horrendous situations like what we are currently navigating, but we will eventually see it. The thing is, you just don't know when, or where it is going to come from. Engaging in authentic prayer and speaking to G-d from your heart opens the door for kindness to enter our lives and becomes a powerful source of comfort.

About The Author

Coach Ratner Coach Ratner was a world-class rare coin dealer & real estate developer in America. He has now transitioned himself into an influential educator for institutions seeking inspiration. His focus is on fostering meaningful relationships, building self-esteem, and providing spiritual motivation.

The Coach Ratner Podcast is available on
YouTube, **Spotify**, **Apple**
and wherever you listen to your favorite podcasts.

To book Coach Ratner, you can reach him at
CoachRatner@gmail.com.

For those of you who want to get up close and personal, you can find him weekly at the
Aish Essentials program
in the Old City of Jerusalem,
or at **www.CoachRatner.com**.

Preview for

Sunscreen Love

What is the difference between complete and finished?

If you marry the right person, you're complete.

If you marry the wrong person, you're finished.

Start Here

**In the morning
I found her sleeping on my front porch.**

A few hours later, I was on the phone with the county police, trying to prevent a tragic suicide attempt on the side of the highway. This came after days of her relentless calls—every 30 seconds, day after day.

She used my hide-a-key to let herself into my house, rummaged through my home office, and wrote a $20,000 check to herself from my checkbook. She left it on my desk, almost as if she wanted me to find it. I don't think she ever intended to steal the money. The check was her way of telling me she was unraveling mentally. And that might be putting it mildly.

I hesitantly walked into my bedroom, half-expected to find a severed horse's head on my pillow.

This is what happens when you can't define love.

The breakup came after just two months of dating. I knew I was a good catch, but not one worth dying for. I know what it feels like to be dumped—it's a constant, gnawing ache in your gut, and the only remedy is time. Emotions aren't something you can quantify or display for others to understand; they're internal, and only you truly know how deeply the pain hurts. You can't pass that feeling onto someone else. That's why there's no such thing as an easy breakup. However, the pain of a divorce will be exponentially worse than any short-lived relationship.

When the relationship does not go as you had dreamed, it feels like the world is crumbling around you.

At our core, we all strive for the same thing, whether we're fully aware of it or it's buried deep within us: a loving, passionate relationship that lasts a lifetime. I genuinely believe that everyone reading this book has a real chance to achieve that. But the truth is, only a few will reach that point. It takes mental discipline, the ability to control your emotions, and the willingness to be vulnerable and let someone into your heart.

Being in love means two people opening up to one another, sharing their thoughts and feelings, and, more importantly, being emotionally open for each other.

When we're young, love isn't something we think much about. But by our late teens, the idea of dating starts to become a reality. Have you ever heard of anyone taking a class on dating and marriage before diving in? Probably not. Most people approach it through trial and error, hoping for the best. But when it comes to making one of the most important decisions of your life, would you really want to rely on hope and luck? That sounds almost insane.

Much of what we know from marriage comes from what we experienced growing up in our homes. If our parents had a healthy marriage, then we have something good to emulate. If not, we might need to put in more effort to cultivate a healthy relationship of our own.

Another place we get an idea of what marriage is supposed to look like is from romantic comedies and Disney movies. Unfortunately, movies give us a misleading sense of what marriage truly is. Think about it—what's usually the final scene in a romantic comedy? The wedding. Why don't they ever show the couple 20, 30, or even 40 years after the wedding? Because it wouldn't be a romantic comedy, it would be a murder mystery! The reality is, Prince Charming isn't going to magically fix everything in your life, despite what these stories suggest. If you're always holding out for the "perfect" prince or princess, you might never commit, constantly believing that ideal person is just around the corner. This mindset could be why people are marrying later in life, or sometimes not at all.

Has access to internet dating increased your chances of finding love? Maybe, maybe not. The ease of access to endless options can make people more selective—quick to dismiss someone for being a few pounds overweight or having a tiny pimple on their nose. With so many alternatives just a swipe away, it's tempting to find any small excuse to keep searching, even when you've met someone who could lead to a deep, passionate relationship.

We may falsely believe that having multiple dating options actually makes it easier to choose one that we're truly happy with. In reality though, the abundance of options actually requires more effort to make a decision and can easily leave us feeling less satisfied with what we choose. This phenomenon is known as the Paradox of Choice.

It's kind of like going to a restaurant with an overwhelming menu–how many times have you ordered the chicken marsala, only to immediately regret not trying the salmon teriyaki? In theory, you love the large menu, but then you are never satisfied with what you ordered because there were so many other good choices. This is why it is called a paradox.

This concept was popularized by American psychologist Barry Schwartz.[10] Schwartz has long studied the ways in which economics and psychology intersect. He became interested in seeing the way that choices were affecting the happiness of citizens in Western societies. He found that while we have far more options than people did in the past, consumer satisfaction hasn't increased as much as traditional economic theories would predict.

Marriage rates in the U.S. have steadily declined since the early 1970s. The peak occurred in 1946, with over 16 marriages per year per 1,000 people. By 1973, that number had dropped to 11, and today it sits below 7 marriages per 1,000 people annually.

Dating used to be simpler: if you met someone nice with a steady job, you married them. Today's singles are less inclined to settle for someone they would have considered a good match in the past.

This is why understanding the different stages of love is essential—not only for having a more fulfilling relationship, but also for making it easier to find love in the first place. Will reading this book guarantee that you'll find love? No, but it will guarantee that if you're open to learning the 4 Phases of Love and allow yourself to be vulnerable, you will significantly increase your chances of finding a meaningful connection.

It's just like anything else in life—if you don't know the steps, you're more likely to give up. Imagine taking a yoga class for the first time, and the instructor only teaches you how to do downward dog. Technically, you know a yoga pose, but without learning the variety of poses, your practice will never truly develop, and whatever joy you initially had for it will eventually fade. The same applies to

---

[10] The Paradox of Choice: Why More is Less. Ecco Publishers

relationships. If we don't understand the phases necessary to cultivate true love, we risk falling out of love with our partner or spouse, ultimately becoming another failed statistic.

We often believe we understand love and can succeed at it with the knowledge we have. Yet, as marriage and divorce statistics show, it's far more challenging than we realize. No couple walks down the aisle expecting to become part of those statistics. Don't leave the success of your relationship to chance—take control of building the love you truly desire.

In the Western world, the divorce rate hovers between 50% and 60%. However, consider the marriages that don't end in divorce—how many of those couples would describe themselves as being in a happy, passionate relationship? Let's say it's around 50%, which is probably generous. This means that if you're currently in a relationship, whether married or not, your chances of enjoying a lasting, passionate, and fulfilling connection are less than 25%. These statistics are disheartening, and this book is dedicated to helping change that.

We will break down love into four distinct phases. Understanding each phase will assist you in the ongoing development of your relationship. Once you've completed one phase, you'll shift your focus to the next, guiding you through the journey and helping you avoid the critical mistake of marrying the wrong person or staying in a toxic relationship.

Most people can navigate the first three phases, but that's not the primary goal of this book. It's the fourth phase that will lead you to the bliss you've always dreamed of, reminiscent of those fairy tales about princesses and Cinderella.

Phase 1:
The Crush Phase

This typically emerges generally after a few dates. If you don't feel a spark or develop a crush on the person you're dating by then, it's likely time to move on. This initial attraction, often referred to as infatuation, carries a slightly negative connotation, as it can imply that the relationship is driven solely by fleeting physical desire. While this may be true, experiencing infatuation is often a necessary step on the path to the deeper love you ultimately seek. Infatuation can indeed evolve into love, but the confusion between the two can lead many relationships to falter. This book will delve deeply into defining what love really is so you do not end up confusing it with infatuation.

Phase 2:
The Research Phase

This begins when you recognize enough positive qualities in someone to consider yourselves "dating." This is the time for intimate exploration, as you delve into what makes each other tick. What are their likes and dislikes? How do you connect on an emotional level? This stage is thrilling because everything feels new and full of potential. You're eager to learn as much as possible about each other. It's during this phase that you'll assess whether you're ready to commit to a long-term relationship.

Phase 3:
The Commitment Phase

This phase often culminates in marriage, but it can also encompass long-term committed relationships. At this stage, you're both willing to invest the effort necessary to build a future together. Many couples reach this point, but getting here doesn't guarantee anything. Instead of viewing this as the endgame—a common misconception—you should see it as the beginning to a deeper journey.

Think of it like an aspiring athlete aiming to enter a professional sports league, such as the National Basketball Association (NBA). Signing an NBA contract may feel like the pinnacle of success, but it's only the starting line. Now they must perform at a high level week after week to avoid being cut from the team while pursuing a championship. The same applies to marriage; it signifies your entry into the league of a legal commitment, but it doesn't ensure long-term success or happiness. It merely gives you a shot at achieving the ultimate goal: a loving and fulfilling relationship with the same person for a lifetime.

If you want the best chance of experiencing the relationship of your dreams—the kind you see in movies and read about in romantic novels—you'll need to embrace and learn to live through the final phase.

Phase 4:

Never Leaving

This phase represents the pinnacle of your relationship—the most fulfilling and pleasurable stage. Here, your significant other becomes the central focus of your life, and you live with the clarity that nothing can stand in the way of your bond. Every decision you make reflects consideration for their feelings and well-being. This deep connection typically develops after many years of marriage.

While the Commitment Phase and the Never Leaving Phase may seem similar, a significant distinction exists between them. People can be committed to various aspects of life—until they're not. Your commitment can wane or even disappear entirely. Consider how often you've felt dedicated to something, only to lose that commitment later. Beyond romantic relationships, think of times you may have drifted away from commitments to fitness, healthy eating, a favorite sports team, or even a political party.

In contrast, Never Leaving represents the highest level of commitment, where nothing can deter you from being together. You'll stand by each other through thick and thin, persevering through good times and bad. You'll be willing to do whatever it takes to keep your relationship as your number one priority.

This is the ultimate goal of this book: to guide you toward a state of the ultimate bliss. It's the moment you realize both of you are wholeheartedly committed to nurturing a happy, passionate relationship—when you reach the point of *Never Leaving*.

Now available

on Amazon

www.ingramcontent.com/pod-product-compliance
Lightning Source LLC
Chambersburg PA
CBHW071841080526
44589CB00012B/1081